C000230246

Salena Godden has been described as 'The doyenne of the spoken word scene' (Ian McMillan, BBC Radio 3's The Verb); 'The Mae West madam of the salon' (The Sunday Times) and as 'everything the Daily Mail is terrified of' (Kerrang! Magazine). *Under The Pier* a pocket-size pamphlet was published by Nasty Little press in 2011 and her crowd funded literary memoir *Springfield Road* with Unbound Books in 2014.

Salena tops the bill at literary events and festivals nationally and internationally. She appears regularly on a variety of BBC Radio programmes including The Verb and Saturday Live. Working alongside award-winning radio producer Rebecca Maxted, Salena has produced and presented two radio documentaries, *Try A Little Tenderness – The Lost Legacy of Little Miss Cornshucks* and *Stir it Up! – 50 Years of Writing Jamaica* both for BBC R4.

Fishing In The Aftermath – Poems 1994-2014 marks twenty years of poetry and performance and the majority of the work included here is previously unpublished in book form.

Birdkawski xx

Fishing in the
Aftermath

*To Georgia
With Psg love*

SALENA GODDEN

Poems 1994-2014

[signature]
xx

Burning Eye

Fishing in the Aftermath
Poems 1994-2014

Contents

Foreword

Salena Godden is a true renaissance artist; a writer, poet, lyricist, songwriter and performer who helped to bring poetry into clubs in the mid-nineties and back into the public's awareness in the twenty-first century with her radio appearances and Book Club Boutique nights. I met Salena in Cherries Bar in Hastings in 1995 when I was 17. Cherries was an extraordinary pub the likes of which I've not seen since. Happy Hour lasted all day with pints at just a pound. Speed could be purchased behind the bar, joints were openly smoked, fist-fights would often break out and pint glasses were regularly thrown from the balcony onto the road below. Cherries was later shut down and its naked and unarmed owner shot dead by police in his bed.

I had heard she was a poet and as I'd been making attempts at something approximating poetry, I was eager to be introduced, though somewhat daunted by her undeniable presence. Her appearance was strikingly bohemian; in a nightdress and silver trousers, her turquoise eyes met mine. I necked some of my alcoholic concoction and extended a rubber fisting-gloved hand.

"A pleasure to make your acquaintance, my name is Oliver Spleen."

"I'm Salena Saliva." She said and noticing me pour the rest of a quarter bottle of whiskey into my pint of snakebite added, "We shall be drinking partners for life."

I thought it significant that we had both given ourselves visceral surnames and after some talking we both concluded that we'd met a kindred spirit. She took my hand and pulled me across the road to the sea where we ritualistically threw stones into the water to rid ourselves of any past regrets we might have had. After much talking and drinking Salena summoned me through the streets of Hastings chalking on every available wall the words *Saliva and Oliva*.

I invited her back to my parent's home where I read her my bad poetry. She was constructive. Giving me tips and encouraging me to write more. Salena became my pathway to taking myself seriously as a writer and performing artist. In time I would follow in her footsteps and head to London as she had done all those years before me; a path and journey that is told in these poems and stories spanning the twenty years of her London life. At her shows and readings I would avidly watch her perform. Always transfixed in the front row I memorised all the lyrics to her songs and sang them back to her, absorbing her uniquely independent sprit like a sponge.

When I fell ill with HIV-related TB, Salena was regularly at my side with books and music. Without her I'm quite certain I wouldn't have written my book, *Depravikazi* nor had the confidence to form my first band The Flesh Happening. The collection you have in your hands tells the story of her journey, her loves, her hopes, the good times and the bad. It is the journey of a truly driven creative soul into a world of new experiences. Always striving to extract the very marrow of what it is to be alive.

Oli Spleen,
London, February 2014.

Introduction

It was the beginning of the 1990's when I finished college and moved from Hastings to London. I wrote letters to the publishers and record companys that were putting out the books and records I loved and I roamed the streets of the West End knocking on stage doors asking for work. Eventually I was offered a job working up in the flies, backstage at The Theatre Royal Drury Lane, during the production of Miss Saigon. Working in the flies was physical work, you were up in the rafters, pulling the ropes to bring in backdrops and scenery throughout the performance. But theatre hours were perfect for a young poet. Working only during the Theatre's show time, allowed me to have my days free to pursue writing and music, to read books and get to know the capital. Eventually I went to a job interview with Acid Jazz Records. Their offices were located on Tin Pan Alley, their acts like Jamiroquai and The Brand New Heavies were topping the charts, and I was keen to the learn about producing records. So aged just twenty, I landed my first real day job as Acid Jazz A&R assistant. This was also my last day job, I haven't had a regular nine to five job since.

I first appeared on a London poetry stage in 1994 and for the remainder of the 20th century I went under the moniker Salena Saliva. That first ever gig was one warm summer evening upstairs at The Paradise Bar in Kensal Rise, at the invitation of Jock Scot, the notorious mod poet. Jock Scot was the first person I'd interviewed for my monthly *Unsung Heroes* column in the Acid Jazz Magazine. Jock took me under his wing, I remember with fondness his rock and roll influence, that he gave me books and introduced to me to artists like the late Ian Dury and The Blockheads, Shane McGowan, Davy Henderson and The Nectarine No.9. It was Jock Scot who gave me my first ever Bukowski and I was soon collecting and reading everything I could find by the man and others published by Black Sparrow Press. I was so excited by this poetry that I wrote a letter to America, but I missed the boat by a few months – Charles Bukowski died on March 9th 1994, aged seventy three.

Following that first gig at The Paradise, I cut my teeth at weekly events that included Paul Lyalls Excess Express, The Hard Edge Club run by Joe Cairo and Mick P's Pull My Daisy. I remember opening for John Cooper Clarke at Dirtbox – Phil Dirtbox's notorious club in Soho – and performing shows at various raves and clubs like The Ministry Of Sound for Arthrob supporting the likes of Irvine Welsh and Will Self. I'd perform sets of poetry to break-beats and drum and bass instrumentals with DJ Delruby on the decks beside me.

During those early years I wrote many letters to publishers and magazines, Rebel Inc and Canongate were high on my hit list. I used to post packets of poems, using a fountain pen and different colour ink cartridges for each letter, but the reply was always a friendly rejection along the lines of *no matter how many colours of ink you have, we just aren't publishing poetry right now, Salena.* But at least they replied, and my perseverance paid off when they published me in *The Fire People* anthology. It was edited by Lemn Sissay and he invited me to Edinburgh to read at the launch. That week I was asked to do a reading supporting Howard Marks, it was around the time when *Mr Nice* was first published, and I remember having the most wonderful time.

Meanwhile, back in Soho, there were regular poetry nights for *Rising* magazine on D'arblay Street at the Tactical Bar with Tim Wells. And during those years we were all doing shows together, I remember gigging alongside the likes of Murray Lachlan Young, Tim Turnbull, Jennie Bellestar, Francesca Beard, JC001, Patience Agbabi and Lemn Sissay to mention just a few.

It was the 1990's and Soho was my playground. I loved those years in that A&R job, geeky as it sounds, I enjoyed going to the pressing plant to cut vinyl. I was asked to wine and dine new bands and was out watching gigs every night. I took it quite seriously, I understood it cost money and took courage to send in demos and so I'd listen to each and every cassette tape and write the bands a letter so at least they'd had a reply and some help.

It was the summer and I asked my boss Eddie Piller if I could A&R Woodstock. I told him I wanted to seek new talent emerging in the states and go to the 25th anniversary of Woodstock on the original site of Yaskurs Farm. I had been invited to tag along with an unsigned band called Spanglehead. Woodstock changed my life, after the festival finished, this adventure escalated into a hedonistic Hunter S Thompson inspired road trip across the US, from New York, through Texas into Arizona. When I finally returned to England it was already September. I was black from the desert sun, fuelled by tales of Timothy Leary's kitchen and galvanised from meeting Hopi Indians. I wish I had a copy of the resignation letter I submitted to Eddie when I got back, I'd print it in here if I could. As much as it was innocent and romantic, it was a declaration to give my whole life up to writing, inspired by the freedom I'd discovered on the open road and not once in the last twenty years have I regretted that decision.

I understood the writing life wasn't an easy life, I had to learn to hustle. Poetry is not for the fame hungry or the lightweight. I believe every book should lead you to another book, every author to other authors. Reading is the gateway drug to writing. The influences of Jock Scot and Tim Wells, John Cooper Clarke and Charles Bukowski lead me to discover John Fante, Richard Brautigan, Carson McCullers and Flannery O'Connor. I spent a lot of time in the public library to nourish my appetite for reading and to find solitude. It was a place to keep warm in the winter and also the cheapest place to photocopy new poems to post to my hit list. Back then there was some method in the madness and a fierce discipline through the booze and chaos. It takes guts to stand by your convictions and to this day my advice to any young writer is taken from Churchill: never, never give up. My only other advice is: don't ask for advice, listen to yourself.

By 1996 I had met and formed a partnership with composer Peter Coyte. We started a ska-punk band, which after several name changes and band line-ups, was called SaltPeter. The Times heralded us as 'the art school Neneh Cherry' and The Independent 'Lily Allen for adults.' The lyrics were juicy, dark and dirty served with Peter's inimitable filmic melodies and drum and bass. As well as independently producing our own CD's and appearing at festivals in and around Europe for over a decade, we also made 'SaltPeter Radio' for BBC. Following on from this, I produced an eclectic weekly show on Resonance FM for several years alongside Marcus Downe which promoted the poets, writers and the musicians on the scene, buskers and people we found on the street. It was like a party live on air every week. During the late 1990's I was introduced to Jon Moore and began recording with Coldcut and Ninja Tunes Records. My poems *Noah's Toilet* and *The Tale Of Miss Virginia Epitome* featured on the *Let Us Play* and *Let Us Replay* albums. Coldcut invited me to perform with them, and before I knew where I was, I was having the time of my life, touring all over Europe and Japan and getting lovely mentions in The Melody Maker and NME. I have not included the lyrics and the poetry from those years with SaltPeter and other collaborations in this collection though, here we'll focus more on the spoken word and page work.

It is with warmth I recall 1994. That summer I was on national television, as a presenter for Glastonbury on Channel 4 where I shook hands with Johnny and June Cash. Around that time I also met the beautiful Jeff Buckley playing down at the 12 Bar on Tin Pan Alley. Kurt Cobain died in 1994 and I distinctly remember that front cover of that Melody Maker.

Poetry was my world, it was loud and ranting in a dark smoky room above a pub, with thick sticky carpets and nicotine stained walls. Now look where we are, it is 2014 and poetry cuts a fine dash and headlines major international festivals; poetry is publishing fiercely and independently; poetry is online and getting hits on youtube and poetry is on the BBC. If you are under a certain age you will take many of these things for granted. I was often the only writer of colour or the only female poet on the bill at gigs, sometimes I still am, but I am thrilled to see this change, to watch the perception of poetry changing, to listen to new voices being heard.

This collection grazes on themes of this writing life, the drink, the sex, the adventure and the after party in all its mess and glory. Some of the early pieces were only ever performed for one show then archived away. Other poems in this book have tattooed me and become party pieces or festival favourites. For the rest of my life I cannot say the word *imagine* without someone somewhere laughing and saying *lick it*. And just like a tattoo, I cannot erase the fact that some of these poems were written from a more self destructive place.

When I was twenty I believed that to be a real writer you had to live dangerously close to the edge, to starve and give it everything you had. I didn't protect myself and I was itinerant, throwing myself at the mercy of the kindness of strangers. I flew from the frying pan into the flame, from war zones to dodgy drinking dens and mad houses. All I can do is thank all my kind and generous friends who invited me to sleep in their houses, gave me bus fare or lent me a winter coat.

There is a fearlessness I find visiting these early poems, I carved this path without a map or compass, often taking a wrong turn, but sometimes luckily remembering to write it down.

These poems are not presented in chronological order. Being in New York to witness the end of the world as we know it changed something, both inside me and outside there. So maybe that is where we can draw a line, the poet before and after 9/11 and the start of the twentieth-first century. Please note I have edited as little as possible of the very early poems to keep the CAPS LOCK style and spirit of that punk-ass poet true to the page.

From the outset this book contains flashing violent images, graphic sex, bad language and fury. It also contains a blatant honesty, tenderness, laughter and all my love.

Salena Godden
London, March 2014

Fishing in the Aftermath
Poems 1994-2014

Dedicated to
The Good Cock

Somewhere in this City

You are there –
you are overworked and underpaid.
You sit at your desk
with a pile of unsolicited post.
We haven't met but I can picture you
and a huge stack of unopened envelopes.
You sigh – oh, where to start?
Come on, let me help you.
Please pick out the one with my name on it.
OK, got it?
Yes. That's the one.
That's the one from me to you.
Put it in your bag and leave the office,
go to the park or the beach or the library
or even better, go to a nice pub and order a beer and a whiskey
and then read my words.
If you get into trouble for bunking off,
tell your boss it's all my fault.
If you get in trouble for drinking,
I'll gladly take the heat.
I will look out for a letter
or even a phone call,
and yes, I'm really looking forward
to meeting you
too.

Tick No Box

There is only one job
where you make so many friends,
have a lot of laughs,
travel the world,
feel so busy and get so occupied,
feel like you constantly have more to learn
and yet seem to achieve so little.

There is only one job
where there is always a long way to go,
mountains to climb,
humble pie to swallow,
so much skying to do,
cloud-bothering and moon-bathing,
hustles and hard knocks,
and that's the full-time job of poetry.

Poetry is the poor cousin
at the wedding of real writing;
journalists and authors and comedians
and playwrights and broadcasters are real writing.
I can imagine this great banquet.
There's poetry sitting on the floor,
begging and feeding off the scraps it is thrown,
a one-minute slot here,
a bit of telly there,
a spot of radio, yeah,
slipped in like an afterthought,
an amuse-bouche, an aperitif,
before the juggler and after the hula-hoop girl.

About once a year a blaggard
writes an article with the headline
'Poetry Is the New Rock and Roll'.
This is swiftly followed by debates about the health of poetry,
as though poetry is an elderly distant relative,
coughing up blood and awaiting test results.
People get excited…
And then it all goes quiet again,
and poetry slumps back to its blogs and the back pages,
by the crossword and an advert to buy thermal long johns.

Poetry is akin to the poi juggler.
You can see it takes some skill and practice,
but seriously, can you be bothered?
Poetry is the failed comedy,
and the indulgent monologue,
the verbose non-song with no melody.
Poetry is all short bony lines with no meat or pictures.
Poetry is hardly ever asked to sit at the big table with real writing,
rarely passed the gravy or the bread,
never given an actual plate or cutlery.
Poetry eats off the floor with ink-stained hands,
bad teeth and absinthe-blind,
because poetry is a dog,
because poetry is a sad orphan,
because poetry is difficult,
because poetry isn't sexy,
because poetry audiences have no attention span
for a poem that is longer than one minute.

And writing sits up high at the big table feasting,
sucking bone marrow and slurping whine and sour grapes.
Hmm, interesting… what is real poetry?
Darling, it must be the poetry that was expensive!
Or the poetry that told the truth,
the poetry that was all about you,
the poem that was all about me, me, me.
Or is it the poetry that the clever person told you was clever poetry?
Or the poetry that paid homage and bowed to the Queen?
Or the poetry of the mad or the poetry of the dead?
Real poetry is dead poetry.
Yes. We all agree.
Dead people write real poetry!

I'd rather sit under the table
than pull up a chair and join the salesmen and magicians.
And I suggest as poets we all carry on,
carry on as we always have and always will do,
carry on doing our writings and doing our readings,
carry on reading, carry on writing, as you were and as you are,
while the big mouths dribble all over the big table,
and decide amongst themselves.

What this is and
who we are and
why we do this.

Poetry.
An odd life is poetry.
I do it on purpose.
This work is all my own work,
working towards changing all of the above,
none of the above.
I tick no box.

The Saturday Shift

I'm trying to read a Jonathan Franzen article,
his opinion of culture and despair.
Bottom line is, he says,
we just don't read enough.

There are two old ladies in this afternoon
with frazzled, dried-apricot hair.
They're ordering double vodkas,
with homeopathic splashes of lemonade.

I'm having a glass of red,
and chain smoking.
It's a warm September afternoon
but I bet old Reg
would have wanted
that fire burning brightly.
He'd insist on more coal and more shush,
raising his long bony finger to his thin grey lips
blue with wine and kissing death.

Reg used to have pints of light and bitter,
but after that visit to the doctor's,
large gin and tonics with plenty of ice.
They can keep things on ice, you know,
until they find a cure...

Kate says we are selling death,
tobacco and booze, she says,
we're as bad as any crack dealer,
what's the difference, she says,
we all do it to ourselves, don't we?

The funeral on Friday,
sausage rolls on a plate,
the regulars wear suits and ties,
us girls behind the bar in black and
we all raise a glass,
we served him his last drinks,
because you cannot catch last orders
transdermally,
and if you only had so much time
would you stay at home alone
with a takeaway in front of the telly?
Me neither.

He was in the pub every day;
we watched his sallow deterioration.
He was swollen-bellied and cold all summer,
a stale perfume of decay,
like a snappy threadbare dog.
But we were used to him, we loved him in our way,
and the fireplace is empty and strange
without him standing there now.

That glass of red went down well,
the old ladies buy me another,
I light a fag,
I do it to myself but
I don't bother to finish the Jonathan Franzen article.
Life is too short and even I know
we should all read more.

Don't Feed the Poets

I keep meeting writers,
artists and musicians
who have given up
writing, painting
or music.
And we get wasted,
we smoke and we drink
and talk of wasted talent,
and it always ends
the same way,
with me insisting
that the colours and
the notes and the words
don't die,
sometimes
they just get lost.
I tell them
I couldn't ever
quit and walk
out on writing.
It's usually then
they give me that look
always that look –
like one day
I will give up
they look at me
like one day I'll see how
hard it is to make it work
they look at me
like I don't get it
like I don't understand
and I stop talking
and I smoke and drink and
think they never did.

Memo: Breathe

I was losing my touch,
losing the feeling in my fingers.
I kept dropping things, hot tea cups,
my fingertips were tingly, fizzing
or completely numb.
I was paranoid I'd start losing fingers and
I was afraid my hands would fall off,
that I'd never be able to hold a pencil again.
I rehearsed trying to type
with a pen sellotaped to my forehead
and I practised writing with my toes.
Then I had to have brain scans.
I had to have my spine pulled straight, my
neck poked and pummelled,
and pins stuck in my feet.
Then there were concerned looks
as all my fears and anxieties
were pushed about
like cold vegetables
on a child's plate
in therapy.
One day the fizz just stopped and
some of the fear went too.
My touch was normal and
my fingers remain firmly attached to my hands
and to my wrists and arms and body.
I don't have to type this with a pen sellotaped to my forehead.
Seems the thing is that –
sometimes I forget to breathe.
Can you believe that?
I forget to breathe, breathe?
Whatever you do with your life,
you have one job,
just one thing to remember:
Breathe.

Emily

I met you on a tube train and asked you
if you wanted to pole dance with me.
You said you did and so you did.
We swung from the bars
on the Piccadilly line,
and then we took you home
and drank cocktails until dawn.
I liked your face,
brown sugared with freckles,
eyes full of mischief and life.

Genuine,
one hundred per cent fun.
You were quick and so smart too,
you had the boys eating out of the palms of your hands.
Your hands were small and soft to hold,
and your nails short and dirty.
Laughing with a mouth full of teeth,
you'd wipe the sleep from the corner of your eye,
and say yes, but of course, everything, the world,
of course, why not?
With you – nothing was too far or too bold.
Your head was full of brilliant ideas
to get us into trouble,
if they ever caught us, caught you.

Now, I remember the sun rising in Islington,
the pavement shone with gold,
and I bawled my eyes out in Angel,
tears before bedtime,
and some broken boy heartache.
It was 7am and you suggested
we go to the postman's pub.
You got us another pair of pints,
lit two fags and quietly
told me it was going be all right.
You see, you had me eating out of the palms of
your hands too.
And you made me see the light and the funny
side.

So I was going to say,
I thought that I'd see you this summer.
I'd smoke all your cigarettes,
laugh about boys,
watch the sun rise,
and bombard you with poetry.
I was going to say
one hundred things,
you lovely, lovely girl.
But words are not enough.
Instead –
I will plainly say,
I will always miss you.

Patti Smith

In a Greek bar, drinking ouzo
in Saint Michel
with a pencilled
moustache
like Dali
I see a familiar figure
in a big coat
woolly hat and spectacles
peering in the window.

Oi Patti!
I holler, chasing her
up the street.
PATTI!
I yell.
Excuse me, are you?

She takes off her glasses
and shakes my hand.
I say,
It would be a great honour
for you to join us for a drink.

So softly
she replies,
Oh man, I can't,
I gotta work
back in my hotel room...

Her voice is so gentle it
throws me
star-struck.

I search my pockets for a gift,
some present to
give her.

I find my black eye pencil
and blurt,
Then can I give you a moustache
like mine?

She looks at my face
and says,
I was kinda
born with one.

A deathly silence.
I say oh
oh yes
yes oh um.

We shake hands
and then
she is gone,
lost in the crowds
of Saint Michel.

Cervical Smear

Open your legs, poke your inner flower.
That's it, lady. Did you bathe or shower
before you came to surgery today?
Looks like you should have, shall we say.

Now see these metal razor-sharp utensils,
as wide as sellotape around one hundred and fifty pencils.
Now, that's to clamp you like a car jack.
Just relax, lie on your back.

Ooh, lady! You are a wide one.
Have you had children or just a good run?
Let me shove in this splintered wood,
ram it in carelessly, oh you are good.

Now breathe slowly while I insert
some broken glass covered in dirt,
and twist and spring catch it wide,
with fourteen mirrors and spoons inside.

There you go, slip back into your clothes.
I place my glasses on my nose.
You'll have the results in a few days.
Try to use lube and not mayonnaise.

Now, what exactly seemed to be the trouble?
A little itch? That's your shaving stubble.
Now, take the Pill until you're forty.
See you then, if you're not naughty.

Next patient please, nurse, there's a sweet,
as I mop Vaseline off my plastic sheet
and sterilise my razor-sharp sticks of lead.
Hello lady, hello lady, hop on the bed.

This Poem

This poem is not designed.
And this poem is not the map.
It is not written to give you something to relate to.
This poem will not be the words you recite to your lover in the night.
This poem will not be the words you scratch
into your prison cell walls with bleeding nails.
This poem is not designed to arouse you or even confuse you.
This poem will not make you laugh or cry or feel.
It will not be the lines that make you remember how to live.
It will not remind you of the time you cut your finger sledging,
as vivid as blood in the snow
and everlasting as the scar made that day.
This poem does not taste like old five-pence pieces,
and it will not sound like an ice cream van in summertime.
This poem will not enlighten you like a Buddhist prayer.
It will not fill you with wonder at the human condition.
This poem will not feed you like potatoes and gravy
and it will not answer your questions of being alone in this.
This poem cannot be your friend
or explain that reoccurring chewing-gum dream.
It will not stop you calling out in the night in cold and acrid sweat.
This poem cannot help you.
It will not inspire you to take up writing or even to continue.
This poem is not the way in or the way out.
It will not feel like winning and it will not feel like losing.
This poem will not make your bus come sooner.
It will not make your cake rise or guess the lottery numbers.
This poem is not written to be anything other than
what you want to read into it,
and if you expect a poem to ever do anything more
then you should read this full stop.

The NYPD and the Model

Officer,
we found him in our bed
naked, tan and toned.
Officer, it wasn't our fault,
we didn't invite him there,
Cherry and I rolled in and
lifted the sheet and there he was.
Officer, when we saw him
our clothes, they kind of fell off,
Officer, and he somehow fell between us.
I think he was lost and cold
and so we warmed him up.

Officer, yes I admit
we were under the influence,
it was dawn and arm-in-arm
we sang our way home from
the Green Point Tavern,
next thing we know
we find this fallen angel
lost in our bed and then
suddenly we were all naked
all three of us
kissing and rubbing
up close and then it all goes blank,

Officer, I honestly do not
recollect anything further,
maybe it was all a dream.
I remember something about a freckle,
somebody's tongue and
a nipple and vague memories
of some kind of fun and some laughing.
Oh yes, Officer, I definitely
recall some laughing,
Officer, but I do not know how he got there,
there in our bed, when we got home,
why, there must be a hole in a
Vogue magazine somewhere,
he looks like he just fell out
of some perfectly lit photo-shoot
for designer underwear
and landed in our bed
all naked and lost and cold and
it was pointing at us and
that's how we found him.
Officer, yes,
we know it's rude to point.
Oh no, Officer,
no sir, we won't let it happen
ever again...

The Last Big Drinky

It started when she finished the radio show last Wednesday, now seven days later there are lines of empty bottles, eighteen vodka bottles, six gin, various litre bottles of Baileys and Schnapps in a row by the bin along the kitchen wall, which is filthy from the food fights. There are plastic bags of crumpled beer and cider cans. She shows me her tongue it is furred green and she says her guts are wrenching, retching, acid. She washes her bed sheets; they are covered in pizza, vodka, fag ash, blood and come. She shows me a note the neighbour upstairs had left asking if everything was alright. He saw the ambulance the other night. It was an accident, the girl with golden hair fell, they were trying to get her to sleep it off a bit in Saliva's bed and she fell face first and smacked her forehead open. It looked like a second right eyebrow, the gash pissed blood everywhere, they had to keep the photographers dog from licking it and you could see deep inside there was something like skull bone or matter.

"I am having a bit of a drinky from this week's radio show through to next." We all heard Saliva announce and that was that. Now Saliva doesn't remember where she put each end of the piece of string, it comes in flashes, could be the beginning or the middle or the end of the story, but I was there for it and one thing is for sure she was in the pub everyday. I also know that really was the last big drinky.

It was a laugh – like when the boys were dressed in her underwear and swimming goggles and they ran out into the street in February's first falling snow. It fell in lovely fat flakes and we joined in and we all danced in the road, holding our tongues out to catch snowflakes. Another neighbour came out and said something about being quiet. We apologised and did try to quieten down but then we soon forgot about that and opened another bottle of frozen vodka playing that song we love. Saliva got a new poem out and Carcass read it aloud in his booming Shakespeare voice and we all fell about laughing.

It was wild that week, like a carefree careless full moon, a lawless restlessness. I kept throwing lemons and tomatoes at Babyblue's head until I was sick. I puked in the bathroom sink and Saliva looked after me. I was going to try and sleep on the toilet but she called me a lightweight whilst pushing my sick down the plug hole with her finger.

"What are we drinking? BBC?" Carcass asked

"No I sold a poem."

"Nice one! So which poem are we drinking then?"

"*I Don't Do Love*. They paid cash into my account, thirsty?"

Saliva orders another round of black sambuca and pints to chase.

34

"Here's to *I Don't Do Love*," Carcass bellowed, "*you don't do love, loves does you.*"

"Yeah love does me, now lets all have a drinky... for a week."

It was that winter dusk light when she phoned me wondering if she had slept all night or all day and then she didn't know which day or time it was. Saliva had woken up twitching, she has a vodka orange whilst she brushes her teeth, she says the mint toothpaste would make the orange taste shit so she brushes her teeth with vodka. She washes her face in ice cold sparkling water and says the bubbles keep her young looking. She wore yesterday's suit with tomorrow's shirt and she stopped at the off licence to pick up a bottle of vodka, cranberry, couple of bottles of fizzy and two packets of cigarettes on the way to the pub so she wouldn't miss closing on the way back. She sat at the bar and talked to the barman holding her pen erect. She had her notebook open to write, but the barman kept talking to her and she kept answering him. She wanted to write about this dream she had had about the rose petals she had been collecting in pint glasses in rows around the skirting boards of her flat but instead all she scribbled in large curly letters is a new word she'd made up – Vodrosekapetal.

"It's funny! Taste this, Malibu, tastes like suntan oil." She says to me and she smirks dirtily and says it tastes like sun tan lotion and drinks it anyway and orders another because it tastes like holidays. That was the night Saliva invited the golden haired girl back with everyone else, including me, Babyblue and Carcass, Saliva invited half the pub back to hers, as usual everybody back to Saliva's. The photographer, the barman, Buddhist lady, the butcher, the baker, the candlestick maker, there were loads of us in the flat. The golden girl, poor thing, she had to have eight stitches we found out in the pub the next day when we were all having brunch-time pints of Bloody Mary.

People came and went that week, it was like Paddington station but timeless and continuous. Sleep? I remember passing out when the room was a haze of grey smoke and that blue light of dawn was seeping through a crack in the curtains. Babyblue and Saliva went to bed together to have sex they won't remember. She likes it though because she loves fucking Babyblue. He's a beautiful six foot six, twenty year old boy the colouring of honey and summer hay bales and he loves Saliva. He lives in what she calls the treats and surprises compartment of her head, the good times chamber in her life, they only do good times together, nothing heavy or committed. They hook up to have a laugh, have a fuck and drink and that suits them both fine.

35

2.

Someone puts Iggy Pop's *I Wanna Be Your Dog* on nice and loud. I had crashed with Carcass at my feet like a wolfhound. We take a pinch of snuff, pour morning vodka oranges down us and spring back into a new drinky. That was the day we went drinking around Camden all afternoon and on leaving The Good Mixer near closing time I watched Saliva in the market on Inverness Street. There were rotting discarded peaches and apricots in the gutter and decomposing grapes and squashed tomatoes. She shouted to the night sky, she said the sky was just an old black blanket with moth holes of sunlight,

"We are not even as clever as ants, we are tiny little human nothings, bacteria, even the stars are distinguishing, the stars are distinguished." She laughed out loud to herself saying she meant to say extinguished and on the other side of the street I saw a little girl in a red coat tugging on her mothers hand, as they hurry past she says, "Mummy look at the funny lady."

"Don't stare dear."

Back at Saliva's we fall out of a cab none of us remember getting into. That was when Saliva got us to lay on the bed and she showered us, threw those pints of rose petals all over our faces. It was snowing outside and inside with rose petals, it was beautiful, glass upon glass of soft fresh rose petals. A petal soaked in vodka on your tongue that's a vodrosekapetal, Saliva kept saying, vodrosekapetal, vod-rose-ka-petal...and then somebody made noodles. They are half eaten in fistfuls but mostly thrown around, hilarious as they stick to your face, splat to your cheek and the ceiling, there is a weird smell as the light bulb fries noodles, the wooden floorboards are covered in a carpet of wilting petals and ripped fruit and pips like the market on Inverness Street whilst the windows are battered with heavy snow. Mushrooms and red rose petals, they taste good together, we eat Mexican liberty caps wrapped in red rose petals.

Me and Saliva start sucking noodles off his belly. Kissing me and Saliva kisses him and then we three kiss and there is that electricity of anticipation and so we say shall we? Then we say we shall. Kissing and stumbling into the bedroom to roll around the bed until daylight is a sodden blur of breathy exchanges and oily bodies and then we pass out exhausted, covered in a fog of drunken sex with the first shards of sunlight streaming through the wide open window. Waking up he lifts the white duvet to see it was not a dream, entwined and naked, we are a six legged animal. Saliva gets up and says

"I think this calls for a drinky! Coffee is what normal people drink in the morning!" She laughs, naked and swigging at a litre of Baileys. "Nice, try it...bit like coffee and drinky to go."

Saliva is in the middle...I can feel both fingers slipping in and out together...three fingers slide and caress inside...we look into our eyes and faces and we nod and are in this...and we are...and we take it in turns, curling tongues around the skin...as if underwater...and in slow motion...we are an octopus and we move over and under each other...we become a pit of snakes...it sounds like feeding time at the zoo...we are greedy...filled... filling...at the same time...and on all fours but on six legs...feeling it slapping softly against fingertips...a timeless place...the possibilities for pleasure seem endless...we are three...rolling over each other, under each other and into each other's arms...with legs bent and legs straight and legs thrown over shoulders and mouths and gasps until...rub it in and splutter and laugh...and it's time for a little smoky and a little drinky.

We talk sitting, upright cross-legged, under the sheet like a white tent...daylight passes into night and then dawn again in this soft feathery place with glasses of frozen vodka and orange...a careless white underworld...a lawless place...we smoke blue smoke...caked in wet petals and outside it snows and fat snowflakes fly onto the bed and we peek out from the covers into the courtyard at the flurry, at the white trees and rooftops and we find the white world outside is inside and it's a beautiful place...we are in love there and then... in that very moment...we decide to get married...the three of us and then...we discuss sticking a lemon up there...pinned between them... squealing ticklish and wriggling whilst they take it in turns to... kissing each other at the same time...we are putting on fishnet tights which are ripped at the gusset...sighing and holding hands...taking it in turns slowly...we tie him up...he ties us up...we are kissing...he is watching...it's ridiculous...it's twister and hysterical...he is coming... laughing and blind-folded...he is delirious...we are cock-drunk...he is cunt-blind...he kneels in front of a spaghetti of ripped fish-netted legs coming out of a snowdrift...four legs in a meringue...three tongues catch snowflakes...two cunts held open by thirty fingers... one cock crowing in the dawn and coming over a million hairs.

3.

It's chronic daylight and Saliva and I drink cold tins of cider and the phone won't stop ringing. She lights a fag, takes a deep breath and answers and it's a one-day workshop job, she says it's been cancelled. Saliva, she doesn't care, she is not convinced she will be able to tell kids how great a poet's life is by tomorrow, let them figure it out for themselves. The phone rings again, it's a bit of telly, they want an interview and a poem. Saliva says she won't do it for free, I am smoking a fag listening as she pulls faces and hand gestures *wankers* at the phone receiver.

"What is it with you Media types anyway?...I know how this goes...it goes like this first you will tell me that it's just a little chat and a poem...then you will edit my shit so I fill your polemic and tokenism...AND you'll try to justify your salary by getting creative on my shit but ask me to do it for free, you will tell me it's for my CV."

Saliva is like a caged tiger, she pounds the floor stretching the phone line and says, "CV? Have you seen my CV? I will have to suffer you crudely cutting and editing my work and the good lines will be edited out because they are too RUDE, what is rude? And why do you people persist in coming to me in the first place? You should go and get Pam Ayres, she's clean, why come to me when you know my work and have seen me...SOMETIMES I CAN BE A RIGHT DIRTY BITCH! GO GET PAM AYRES!. PAM AYRES IS FAMILY FUN. What? What do you mean? You people treat poets like ordering pizza, you say you like it but instead of cheese can you have custard? I will have to tell you over and over custard and pizza don't work, but you think you know all about poetry and you will argue with me armed with the bit of Hughes and Plath you had to do in school...instead of cheese let's have custard you will repeat having lured me out to dinner on expenses at Soho House. You'll sit there thinking you are my editor. Then you will film me some place humiliating like on an open-top tourist bus in Oxford Circus at rush hour and wonder why it doesn't resonate with the same delivery as when you saw me read in the Colony Rooms...to add insult to injury you will spell my name wrong in the credits...and you'll probably phone me with insipid and ridiculous suggestions like you'll suggest using toffees and marbles instead of mushrooms and buttons and blackberries instead of olives and shampoo instead of tomato sauce, like now all of a sudden you know all about pizzas? Now you know all about poetry? And I get to do all this for free? You've got your commission right? Are you doing your job for free? Is the camera-man doing it for free? Is this BBCharity? Channel Poor? I bet there is money in the budget for everything, your colonic irrigation, your humour bypass, your Christmas in Goa but the monkey on the screen, ME I do it for ZERO DOLLAR...then I get stopped and frankly harassed in the pub by some smart arse, they say, have you ever tried using pepperoni on pizza because they saw ME on telly using pennies for sausage and I will have to tell them it was YOUR stupid idea and YOUR edit that used PENNIES instead of PEPPERONI...but its ME on the idiot box flipping over and over like the funny monkey, so come on throw me a peanut, why don't you peel me a banana? And?....Yes please, you do that, you check the budget...pennies instead of pepperoni I don't think so chump... check with the boss and then you get back to me....thanks.

"Was I a bit rude to me-me-me-dear, meeja lady?" Saliva asks. We walk having left the house abruptly before the phone can ring again. "I think saying I am a dirty bitch go get Pam Ayres was a bit strong!" We snigger about custard on pizza, pennies for pepperoni and drink cider walking to the job centre.

4.

The place is fast and noisy with queues of non-activity and Saliva goes in wearing a purple bowler hat, swigging a tin of cider, swaggering and grinning. We fit in, covered in handprints, bruised love bites and bed hair, we are twinned by the dreadlocked clumps at the back of our heads. We fit in with the alcoholics and junkies and mental cases. It's in part both hilarious and terrifying now the magic mushrooms are wearing off. We look like crack whores, stinking of booze and sex. We cannot walk upright or straight. When we look at each other we keep sniggering. The woman behind the desk gives Saliva a grilling; she made a mistake wearing the purple hat, the fur coat and the idiot grin. It's too hot and we are sweating booze profusely, we shift in our seats nervous to get out of there. The woman is suited and officious and she asks, "What have you done to seek work in the last two weeks?"

Saliva tells her she is waiting for her agent to get back to her publisher to get back to her manager who is waiting to get the contracts from the lawyer.

"And?"

"Oh and...I have been sending out my work...reading the papers...checking the Internet and stuff...I got a telly offer today, this morning, actually and I am just waiting for them to get back to me ... regarding pizza...I mean budget..." Saliva squirms unconvincingly. The New Deal Advisor sniffs, tapping the keys of the computer with her talons and we know she knows we know she can smell the good time on us.

We head into the first pub we pass, it stinks dark and creepy, the barkeep looks odd and unfriendly. We get a pair of halves just to give us the strength and energy to get to the nice pub Saliva says. A urine drenched, puke covered old man with a red face sits opposite us and won't stop laughing. We laugh with him for a minute, he laughs and says something and we nod pretending to understand and he laughs again repeating whatever it is he says. Snot comes out of his nose in a bubble, then he coughs up something like a chunk of cottage cheese. Saliva downs the remainder of the half, stands and hurriedly leaves the pub to retch into the gutter with repulsion.

"You OK?" I ask lighting her a fag

"I felt the tramp, its surreal, like I felt his very soul, his life or some weird vibe…it was disgusting." Saliva tells me. We walk towards the nice pub, but every time Saliva remembers his face and his cough up, she grits her teeth and fights to hold in her stomach contents.

In the nice pub we watch the snow outside and it's warm by the fire. We have a laugh and a drinky, pints of spritzer are followed by vodkas and sambucas and lots of joking about the faces we pull and the noises people make when they have sex. And then something about music and who wrote that song? We forget but we hum along and random people, strangers come and sit with us and so Saliva gets them shots too. London is thirsty, good because we are having a drinky, Saliva keeps saying, let's drink love. She tries to drink without using her hands and accidentally bites the glass. I freak and stand up ready to mop blood, Saliva's mouth is full of glass but she isn't hurt or cut. She grins at me and picks chunks and shards of glass out of her mouth, rinses her mouth out with booze and spits it on the pub floor.

A mad woman sits with us, she has been in prison three times. She has the remains of two black eyes where police beat her up in the back of a van. She has been abused all of her life she says. Saliva gets her a whiskey. The mad woman says she has two beautiful daughters and she went inside because one of her daughters married a wife beater and she nearly killed him for it. You don't hurt my girls and get away with it she says time and time again. She is getting wound up, she says she is violent; she says she is always angry. Saliva catches a glance with me and we wonder if she is about to kick off, I am ready to grab the ashtray and lump her if she kicks off at Saliva. She is spitting as she speaks, lurching and leaning over us and getting more and more excited. Her arms are tattooed and her teeth broken, she says nobody takes the piss out of me and gets away with it, you'll all get yours, she spits and points one of her fat tobacco stained digits in our faces. Saliva suddenly stands up and makes the woman cuddle her, there in the middle of the pub, she cuddles this frothing mad woman and she kisses her face. Saliva won't let go of the rigid mad woman, she holds her telling the mad woman over and over that she is magic, a lovely and special lady and the mad woman crumbles and starts weeping. Saliva licks and wipes her tears, telling her she is ace, a brilliant woman, and the mad woman breaks down into sobs and says nobody has said a kind word like that to her ever before.

5.

"Can you see the rainbows around the street lights?" Saliva repeats all the way home. We are walking in the snow, the roads are quiet, the street lights make everything orange.

Once we are inside we manage another bottle of vodka and pass out in our clothes. Saliva writhes with horrific nightmares and terrors, she screams in her sleep with seven days of alcohol in her thick syrupy blood. She says there are faces of people looking over the bed and knocking at the windows. She is trying to sleep but all she says she can hear is her heart struggling to beat, she twitches, rocking and flinching in and out of consciousness trying to remember to breathe. We are both aching all over inside and outside, covered in huge black, purple and red bruises from all the rough and tumble, the bundles and the love bite fights. She is drenched in cold acrid sweat, and fear, terrible fear. She says she is unable to move, if the monster comes she won't be able to fight it. In a tiny voice she says she is dying, she says this is what dying feels like, she is falling off the world, she says, and she begs me to never let go of her hand while it is still so dark. We share the fear and holding my hand she is begging to be held convinced she will stop breathing. She says vodka and cock will kill her in the end and she feels as though she is rotting.

By lunchtime we manage to get out of bed, her t-shirt damp with night sweat and there are still three bottles of vodka in the freezer. The walls and floors are sticky and caked with booze and food fights and spilt puddles of noodles, brown petals, cranberry and orange juice. We both get hot flushes trying to clean up and my tongue is kind of bleeding. I make her eat an egg and run her a bath, hearing her puke and piss shit. Terrible panic and paranoia both to go outside and afraid to meet the devil that is here inside, she jumps at shadows and her own reflection in glass. She vomits the egg up and curls in a ball on the sofa covering her face with hands and says she is waiting for it to stop, she says her heart keeps speeding up and stopping. She vomits a pint of water and jokes weakly that its like a stomach rinse, she shakes and says she is still hallucinating.

"I don't want to be Saliva anymore, it's crap, I want to go to a church and work with the needy and play tennis and wear white dresses." She sits up and jokes weakly.

Now she has to go and do the radio show in a few hours, it's already getting dark.

"I promise that was the last drinky, that was the last big drinky, that was the last big big drinky." Saliva repeats to herself over and over putting records and CD's into her box for the show.

"That was the last big drinky for a while...the last big drinky anyway, that was a proper seven dayer...but hey the Full Moon Sports Bag boys are my guests this week. I guess I'll have to have a wee sherry with them, before tonight's show, just to warm up a bit won't I? Just a wee sherry or two before the show, not a drinky though, just a sherry. Just a sherry or maybe a port, yes port is much nicer than sherry. You coming with me? Fancy a wee sherry? Or a baby port maybe? You have to come with me because...because that's not like a real drinky is it? That's just having a sherry and that's a different story altogether."

Blue Cheese, Raw Fish and Olives

When I grow up I will actually like olives,
and understand the need for an early bed,
and why I don't have to finish the bottle,
and why poems don't have to rhyme…

Red. Lipstick will suit me and stay on my lips,
I will walk delicately elegant in high heels,
I will have credit cards and generously tip,
I'll wonder if the world is getting younger and discuss how that feels.

Excuse me, madam-lady, strangers will say,
offering me something nice, perhaps a cake slice,
and I will reply in a grown-up lady type way,
Oh no, thank you, that will surely suffice.

When I grow up I will actually like olives,
and while putting cool cucumbers on my tired eyes,
I will eat black ones with anchovies, thinking they taste nice,
like blue cheese and raw fish and all the other grown-up lies.

Do It To Her and Do It For Her

If you are going to do it to her
tell her she is beautiful
make her feel special
and make out
like you never
had it so good.

If you are going to
do it to her
then do it with her
and do it for her

and she'll show you
her way around you
and your way around her

like her body is a map
your fingers
and your tongue
and your cock

will point out
the major cities
stroke the continents
and spank the war zones.

Do it to her.
Do it with her.
Do it for her.

And the earth will spin on its axis
the stars will shatter
you will discover
another universe

and all you have to do
is let her know
she is the world to you
the most beautiful girl
you ever kissed in the galaxy

and for that one night
you both never had it so good.

Do it to her.
Do it with her.
Do it for her.

And in the morning
do it all,
all over again
so tenderly and
before you even
open your eyes,

but leave
before she asks you to
and come back
before she has time
to doubt
the science
and geography.

Galway Dreaming

I watch the gush of life in the May sunshine.
Galway is slow and golden syrup.
I sit outside the same café all afternoon
slowly sipping beers
watching students cavort
like the swallows above the town,
spring sun shines on my face,
I could not be more happy.
My heart leaps like the fish
in the shimmering river
and I let my gladness run free.
I imagine living here in Ireland,
how I would write another book,
a tender and poetic story and
I'd marry a strapping lad
with soft green-blue eyes,
sometimes we'd drink whiskey
and watch the full moon rise,
my cheeks would be pink
and my body a little plump
but my husband would cherish me,
he'd be faithful and steady and strong,
he'd pick me up and make me laugh like a girl.
I'd have a slower heartbeat.
I'd write poems on the beach each morning
and swim a mile in the bay at sunset.
It would be a good and happy life.
London would become a blurred fog,
a memory of bright lights, big talk and speed
and I dream this dream all day,
I dream this dream,
with one slow
exhalation.

Eyes Like Woodlice

She wasn't very nice.
She had eyes like woodlice.
Eyes like woodlice, eyes like woodlice.
Eyes. Like. Woodlice.
Grey with legs splindled and splayed,
thick clumped with mascara.
At least her lashes got laid.

She wasn't very nice.
She had eyes like woodlice.
Eyes like woodlice, eyes like woodlice.
With a face like a slapped arse.
Even her pitta-bread tits wouldn't speak to each other,
clambering to separate, her bad-tempered tits
edged beneath her dank, damp armpits.

She wasn't very nice and
she worked behind the bar,
pulling pints and faces,
turning heads and stomachs,
with her come-to-sick-bed eyes
edged in scarlet red, like a ladybird, found dead.

She wasn't very nice.
She had eyes like woodlice.
Eyes like woodlice, eyes like woodlice.
With an arse like a violent baboon,
the posture of an elderly hunchback,
that pub was suicide central,
patrons found in the toilets in tears
as grown men sobbed into their soured-milk beers,

wishing they had gone to the other pub
where you were served by a girl with a face
like a patted-powdered chuckle-bum,
by happy tits that absolutely loved each other,
that giggly-jiggled like schoolgirl chums,
that were separated by less than a small ant's thumb.

Fishing in the Aftermath
Brooklyn, 13th September 2001

Stranded in New York
and all out broke,
I go to the 7th Avenue
second-hand bookstore.
All I have is my books to sell,
Bukowski, John Fante,
Seamus Heaney's *Beowulf*,
Fitzgerald, Faulkner
and a Richard Brautigan.

He offers $5.50 for the lot.
I say I'm marooned,
I'm from London,
the airports are closed and
the world has gone mad
and so he offers $7.50,
but the *Beowulf* is brand new and
I never even finished
Trout Fishing in America,
I choke.

My hot eyes sting.
I decide to try Downtown
and take the subway to Broadway.
The train is reassuring,
it's packed as usual.
I perk up and decide to visit
a jovial Irish barman,
to see if he'll give me a beer
or that job washing glasses,
but he's not there for dust and
the bar is boarded up.

I'm obstructed by
do-not-cross police tape,
masked TV crews and
emergency sirens like wasps.
The fire station
is flooded with flowers.

Heading back to Brooklyn,
the sun is a smoking red coal
in billowing black smog.
A gentle man smiles at me,
we get off at the same stop.
I tell him I tried to sell my books,
he says he tried to give blood
but they had enough of his type.
We shake hands and go separate ways
but his smile remains with me.

I make a pot of tea
and curl up on my friend's sofa bed.
I learn to tell the difference
between war planes
and rolling thunder.
Then I go trout fishing
and I finish that
Brautigan.

Cabbages Violet and Green in Vases

A scuttle of traffic along the skirting board,
the droppings are currants, teeth marks in butter
are evidence of our rodent roommates.
A saffron and ginger bog-water soup is simmering,
the bread is needed and kneaded and rising,
The kettle is boiled ready for washing of face and socks,
everything smeared with white chalky fingerprints,
everything is dusty with clay and flour.
Outside it's damp with a new fresh chill.
There's the landlord to avoid,
so throw another log on the fire and let's go to bed.
In crisp white cotton we are Peter Pan and Wendy, we laugh,
like it's one hundred years ago, like time never passed,
and it may as well be –
the ink and the blood and the clay
and the wood and the wine are all the same,
my pen scratches paper parchment, my tapping-typewriter
and you a sculptor, with a rasp, a spatula and nimble fingers.
We are a pair of time-travellers, we are bent tarnished teaspoons.

We move together beneath the rustling of aged cotton,
coming alive with the stark crude purple of flesh and heat.
Tomorrow we might find some rent.
And October's sun will haze over yellow apples and harvest,
the leaves will turn to gold and red and saffron.
Yesterday we bought cabbages as flowering foliage for the vases,
but now I'll have to make some kind of cabbage-flower soup.
Because tomorrow we still won't have the heart to eat the mice.

But tonight may we sleep in dreams of golden honey
like centuries never passed and like nothing will change,
let's fall asleep, listening to the rain.
At least we have the cabbages,
violet and green in vases.

When They Took Her Away

When they took her away
she wasn't kicking or screaming.
It was as though
she'd seen it coming,
like she'd been buying time.
I wanted her to shake her fist,
tell us she'd show us one day.
I thought she'd put up a fight
instead,

when they took her away –
they didn't take her away exactly,
but they led her away –
I saw her lips in a silent whistle
she was exhaling with one breath
she was blowing out a candle
at the end of the night.

As she got into the back seat
they protected her head,
she stared straight ahead
and waited patiently
as they secured her seat belt.

She didn't turn her head
to look at us
staring out the window,
but I like to think
I saw the faintest smile
playing in the corner of her mouth
as the car pulled away.

She'll get plenty of bed rest
where she's going,
books and telly
and free hot meals.
It's probably what she needs.

Come to think of it
it's probably what we all need.

Bit of Sweet

He said
that's sexy
as he held the ladle
to my lips
and I drank
and it was
then
he said
that's sexy
when he said
that's sexy
it was sexy
as we sat there
in the woods
by the bonfire
tripping out
on truffles
Rumpelstiltskin
played
slide guitar
and we
ladled hooch
into each other's
mouths
which was sexy
until the pot
was empty
and we were
all drunk
and maybe
I was
desperate
or lonely
or maybe
it was the
warm light
the sun rising
through
the trees
and

the puddles
of gold
on the forest floor
but when we
left the others
and got lost
in fields
of yellow
waist high
in buttercups
we held hands
and all I kept
thinking
was the way
he'd said
that's sexy
and that
glorious
morning
we sat lost
hidden
in a meadow
of long grass.
It was then
when I went to
kiss him
it was then
when he
pulled away
he said he had
a girlfriend
I acted like
I was just joking
but I thought
that's so sexy
bitter sweet
long time
since a boy
withdrew
in time.

If We Went to Bed

I'd be so shy with you,
snort when I laugh,
we'd bang teeth
with goofy grins,
I'd nip your lip and
any blood is embarrassing.

Clumsy with the lights on
under the blanket,
half-dressed with closed eyes,
and to make it cheap
I'd treat you like a kid
from out of town and
easily forgotten.

But I couldn't dazzle you
with a slippy one-night stand,
you'd ask me what I meant,
you'd look at me with my legs
over your shoulders,
an ankle in each of your hands
your slapping balls
thwump thwump
watching yourself go in
and out and in and out and…

I'd be out of my depth,
it's so easy to lie in a
dark drunk bed,
it's so hard to lie
in the sober light
of the afternoon,
you'd see what I meant,
find your reflection
in my eyes and stop.

We'd lie there speechless
and smoke cigarettes
to change the subject.

A Loner in a Crowded Head

I pressed my cheek against
the granite headstone,
buried my face and howled
into my up-turned coat collar,
tracing the lost years with my thumb,
and my own surname etched in stone.

That winter was brutal
and I fulfilled an obligation
to ride the storm in bed,
I knew I would never be
quite the same again.

A bitter snow fell,
my tongue was furred brown
with tea and sympathy
and shit –
if we were ever honest
we'd admit we dislike
the reflections of our weakness
and there's that mean streak we all share,
and I am only telling you this because I care.
And I took some comfort there.

I cried secretly, like a bulimic in a toilet cubicle,
my fingers down the throat of how it troubled me
that love was failing.
I smeared lipstick on a forced smile,
my blood shot and salt eyes,
weakly disguised with slammed tequila.

And as I walked home, alone,
I sheltered in phone-boxes from the rage and fury,
ashamed at all the drama and all this wet on my face.
Sometimes
there really is no space
in the crowd, to grow or change,
and unsent letters clutter like dead leaves.

Old friends, they loved you then,
when you were at their best,
they loved you more,
when you were more or less.

My faded Prince T-shirt
got out of shape.
It didn't shrink,
I grew out of the wash.
We partied like it was 1999
because it was then.

Above me grey dish rag clouds
are swiped across a greasy sky,
mauve and smeared,
with a pale lilac rain.

I pass pubs we once knew
and the flats we shared
where the rent was always overdue.
Where it was always late,
long nights of whiskey and coke,
when the dawn scribbled gold
on powdery walls,
the rising sun colouring
the smoke a shade of amber.

And we ranted and spat like it mattered,
because it did then.
And I am only telling you this because I care.

Now there are babies and debts and deadlines,
filthy habits and foul coughs,
eccentricities, we once found charming,
stain our crooked teeth and leave a sour taste.
We've all put weight on
shoulders to
cry on.

Deep cuts oozed blood as we gripped hands,
swearing to be blood and kin,
wondering who'd go first
necking pills with wine
it was a fragile time
trembling like
a pigeon's throat.

Remember when this was all ahead of us,
and in the morning we'd laugh and say
one day
we'll all laugh
one day
we'll look back on this and laugh one day.

And I took some comfort there.
That there would be
a one day,
and that it would be funny.

I am a loner
Alone in a crowded head
and crowded in a lonely world.
With three grey hairs precisely
and a faded Prince T-shirt
I only wear to bed.

Fuck Tea, Fuck Toast

fuck being safe, fuck playing safe. in fact fuck playing. fuck being careful. fuck giving a fuck. fuck killing it and fuck damping it down. fuck blocking it and clocking in, fuck ticking the boxes and fuck the box. fuck the rehearsals and fuck the show. fuck fuck fuck. fuck doing what's best and fuck being a good girl. fuck being a good boy. fuck routine. fuck the system. fuck money and fuck the banks. fuck the power and fuck the mind fuck mind fuck mind the gap fuck. mind the fucking gap fuck. fuck control and fuck being controlled and fuck being controlling. fuck the dream and fuck the sleep. fuck food. fuck tea. fuck toast. fuck it. fuck being reasonable and fuck being sensible. fuck. fuck holding back and fuck fighting with one arm behind your fucking back. fuck. fuck holding it in and fuck sucking it up and fuck holding it back. fuck holding on to anything. fuck holding your breath. fuck wondering when it's going to begin and fuck wondering if it's over yet. fuck. fuck hoping it's going to start and fuck hoping it will end. fuck. fuck home and fuck there is no such place as home. fuck playing safe. fuck playing at all. fuck being serious about anything and fuck not being serious enough. fuck faking. fuck taking. fuck making all that fucking carry on about some fucking shit you don't even give enough of a fuck about to even give a minute of your fucking time to fucking remember to give a fuck about it, fuck, so why are you fucking cracking on about fuck it all now? fuck fucking fuck… he said.

he said, of course it fucking hurts that's why it's called fucking sun burn, clue's in the fucking name for it right there… and when it hurts you just think, oh it hurts, and then you think so what if it hurts, get on with it, cos what else are you going to fucking do? waste of time that, saying oh it hurts, deal with it, that's why it's called fucking sun burn, cos it's burnt for fuck's sake. look at my sunburn, he said…

does it hurt? I asked…

of course it hurts, it's just pain and being alive has got pain in it. that's life. life is hard and full of things that hurt. wear a fucking crash hat. deal with it. fucking cunts. not you, you are not a cunt… of course. are you laughing? why are you laughing? is it because I'm funny? do you think I am funny? I like your laugh it makes me laugh. can I ask you something? are you wearing contact lenses? am I wearing contact lenses? no, why did you ask if I am? because I asked if you were? they are blue. real blue. yours are kind of blue as well. look see no lenses, just eyeball, poke it if you like, if you don't believe me, poke my fucking eye, it don't hurt. gimme your finger and touch my eyeball, see no contact lens there, just me fucking eyeball.

I am on the tube and the drunk boy on the train is pretty. his eyebrows are pale gold and his lips are loose. the back of his tan neck begs kissing and nibbling. he is convinced he is coming home with me. how come? let's go back one move, ten minutes ago, he got into the train carriage with me. go back another move, twenty minutes ago we talked at the ticket machine. go back further, he was outside the pub and he followed me into the tube station. rushing to catch the last tube to north london. hang on, now go back one more scene about forty-five minutes ago, we were in the same pub. his friend spilt my drink. then insisted on buying me another. then they made us do a shot of something. I laughed and said that was how they got to talk to hot girls, spill their drinks on them and make them talk to them. are you hot girls then? he winked arrogantly. well I haven't heard any complaints lately I volleyed back. well you seem to be talking to us anyway. yes I do now don't I.

closing time. as I was leaving, he, that one, the one with the soft cheeks, flushed with alcohol, the one there, with that one freckle between the bristle and his top lip. imagine that soft cheek and that freckle against your inner thigh... but yes, he leaned over and said lady, take me home with you and I paused and then nodded and yesnoyesnomaybenoyesnoyno no no... he must have only heard the nodding part.

next thing I know... he's adorable.

I mean, the next thing I know, he is following me down the escalators and every few steps he drops his money, pound coins roll across the polished tube station floor. I bend down and pick them up and give them to him and each time after time, he says thank you. thank you. thank you. I laugh and he laughs too. then he puts them back into his trouser pockets full of holes, again and again.

he says, fucking holes. should sew them holes up. you are right, he repeats himself, I fucking should sew them up. do you know I have seven pairs of trousers and do you know all of them have no pockets that work, all got holes, he says.

oh let me sew your trouser pockets, make you pies, soap your back

59

into a lather and gently pet your sleeping head, I think and I smile at him. I like him, I like people with broken teeth, ripped pockets and worn down heels. I love him, I love you and your damaged goods. you are a chink in the china and a tarnished teaspoon. I know that you and me, we could hold onto the torn sails together of a sinking ship and weather a storm and I know we'd find dry land. we could smash up the furniture and throw the splinters on a fire to keep warm. we could blag it, rinse them all and get away with murder. you'd repair some of my fractures. but still match my broken parts. but you could never damage me any more than I already am or my ill-repaired patchwork head would already allow. we'd be good as new. we'd be held together with safety pins and the bitterness of disparage and sour experience would force us to work together, to get along and get on with it. we'd peel the eyes off potatoes and make them chips all good again, eat them on the grand sofa of this journey. and we may as well get comfortable since we are here. we chose the path, we'll find our way eventually, the long way around. darling, I keep picking up stray cats and underdogs, I never learn, I have no umbrella and in london it is raining cats and dogs.

he thinks I will take him home with me. in fact he is sure of it. I am thinking I might take him home too. and for a few stops, I am convinced of it as clapham bleeds into waterloo and chunders into charing cross. we are in central london now. the halfway point, no turning back, or is there? he is beside me, engaged and engrossed in chatting to me about anything and everything. is it too late to turn back?

his eyes are a blue fire, lively as life itself, self-assured and his nature is true to form, a drunk and plucky young man. now there's a truth. I wonder what I will do with him at my house anyway. I picture him in my kitchen and then I imagine him in my bed. then even worse than that, I begin to wonder how old he might be. and once I start thinking that it's a downward spiral. I realise now that he must be much, much younger than me. and worst of all for once it bothers me. that he is so young and wasted. and I don't know his name. I fast-forward to tomorrow morning. daylight ripping open the darkness, morningness screaming onto twisted sheets. sweat and spunk. spit and exchange. tea and toast. headaches and mess. deadlines and socks. conscience and guilt. condoms and awkwardness. emails and phones ringing. lips and eyes.

but what eyes he has, what eyes he has indeed, so blue. they are so blue. it always begins with the eyes and ends, ends with the eyes too remember. lashes fluttering, battering down the doors and walls of my give a fuck. fuck. fuck. tottenham court road. where do you live? I ask him, where do you live? again I ask him where do you live? that was tottenham court road. he mumbles, sydenham. where? sydenham. where is sydenham? he laughs. I ask him again. eventually he replies south east london. then you are on the wrong train. but I am coming home with you. no. you cannot come home with me. yes I can. no you can't. I can. no. I thought I was coming home with you. oh go on. no. oh. oh. oh ok am I not coming home with you then? no. if you get off here you can catch the last train back south just cross the platform and...

gone. the eyes. goodbye blue eyes. goodbye freckle. gone away now. just me and my own reflection and my fucking head going home alone. fuck being sensible. fuck being careful. fuck deadlines. fuck giving a fuck. fuck getting an early night and fucking fuck fuck fuck... fuck tea. fuck toast.

Skying

I found the pelvis of an elk
and a rose quartz rock,
at the foothills of snow-dipped
Bear Tooth Mountain.

The forever blue
absorbing perspective,
my peripheral vision
is eyeballs in my ears.

I hear the endless expanse
and I have seen sky before,
I have exhaled and
felt like I was

blowing the clouds,
sending them to scurry
across all the rose and violet
the setting sun could cough,

and then disappear
into all the orange yolk
the rising sun
could breakfast.

But now it's as though
I see this blue
for the first time
and I am falling into it.

The breeze in the rushes
whispers like water
cools the wet hair
against my neck.

Dry prairie winds
have burnt my skin foreign,
I see faces in the fool's gold
on the rocky bed of the River Bighorn.

Constable once wrote
I have been doing some skying
and I have sat on this rock
in silence since morning.

Eagles soar and I cannot
look anywhere else
but up, it's like watching you
undress for the first time.

I see the whole
of you and I am
so small and
inconsequential.

I want to sit with you
like this all day.
I stare as you grow
the purplish of dusk

in sudden shadows
of the mountain.
I take a bottle out of the
cool river and I drink

to this sunset
and to the moon rising,
as I hear coyotes call
for nightfall.

I'm Gonna Move to Hastings

I'm gonna move to Hastings,
pick up where I left off,
I'm gonna get drunk every day
with drunks who piss me off.

I'm gonna move to Hastings,
become the fancy blow job queen,
get a job in a dirty dark pub
with a broken ice machine.

I'm gonna move to Hastings
where it's two quid for triple house gin,
I'll go mental, crazy-eyed,
wear no shoes and go through bins.

I'm gonna move to Hastings,
sleep with bouncers and not the bands,
in the toilets I'll have fishermen finger me
with tattooed, corn-rough hands.

I'm gonna move to Hastings,
spend my benefits on the booze,
get off with people's boyfriends,
get in cat fights which I'll lose.

I'm gonna move to Hastings,
smoke cheap fags and score shit gear,
get bloated on chips and vodka,
have weird sex beneath the pier.

I'm gonna move to Hastings,
teenage mothers pissing on the street,
white stilettos without irony
blistering on their feet.

I'm gonna move to Hastings
where it's as cheap as chips
and the bad boys, they crack on
even when the condom rips.

I'm gonna move to Hastings,
go as low as high can go,
we all suck on Hastings rock,
it's the hardest rock I know.

I'm gonna move to Hastings,
bed-sit with a vague view of the sea,
sign on the sick, save my medication,
burn these poems, when they burn me.

After the Flop House

With one hand typing
and the other working
inside my underwear,
the blank page
in front of me,
last night's whiskey
in empty guts,
dull headache
and lips weeping
with cold sores,
I come again,
not for the joy of it,
but sheer hopelessness
filling the gap between you and night.

Lying here, like the beautiful syphilitic whore
delirious and cold with sperm,
a rough fuck on a stained mattress,
in a whorehouse on the border of nowhere,
pipe-smoke sticky in tangled hair,
easy to have and to throw away.

This is nowhere,
and this is not Tangiers.
I take notes as I sample
the bare-arsed natives
and local delicacies.
I'm like a hunter of elephant ivory,
gin in one hand,
and cocked gun in the other,
suffering fevered dreams
beneath a mosquito net,
BBC World Service on the radio.

This is London
and it's raining
sex and drink,
men too young in some states
too in a state in any state
and so much free wine.

Like a maniac
I rub myself raw
to fill the hole you left.

This is nowhere
and this is not Paris
but I collect evidence
with Celine and Miller.
I inhale crystal smoke,
develop a taste for it
like a collector of butterflies
with a bent teaspoon
of liquefied flames
and sugared absinthe.

With one hand typing
and the other working
inside my underwear
it's pure
base greed,
it's just
another
come down
cold sore
hangover.

The blank page
is dirtied,
sex and drink,
it rains and pours
and like cold sores
love lasts painfully
longer in books.

Rock and a Hard Place

From Colorado to Arizona,
the blue snow-lit mountains
are Utah red by dawn.

I drive through Salina –
got no license, it's my
first time behind the wheel but
Simple Man plays on the radio.

I remember his breath,
the way he rasped
there you go baby
there you go

baby
as he so
slowly put it all
the way in.

The way in flutters
against my tight jeans
and judgement
a juggernaut honks past.

I remember
the wild fuck,
wild flowers
by the creek

I picked and left in a jar
on his window sill,
knowing they are still
in that state.

Now I sit here
in front of a big hole,
the whole morning is blue
above carmine rock,

and it's a long way down.
I'm at the Grand Canyon,
trapped between a rock and
a hard place.

A Letter to an Air Stewardess Found in the Back of Seat 67A

Dear Waitress Of The Air,
when you are very old, very grey, very blind and very deaf,
disgracing yourself by wetting your tights
each time you sneeze or cough, and then breaking wind
when you call out in pain and confusion,
when you smell weird as yeast spread and sick,
please do tell your meals-on-wheels do-gooder,
care in the community or Help the Aged social worker
and indeed your only contact with the outside world,
that you once refused to lend a poet a pen
on a short flight to Austria for no reason whatsoever.

Tell them it was back then, back then,
when you were a tangerine-coloured air stewardess,
with a ballerina bun, a soft fruit arse,
over-plucked eyebrows and liar eyes.
Tell them how you got quite a little power kick
out of the fact you were not even using it,
that biro, right there, in the tippety tip of your tiptop pocket,
that you were keeping it there to look official
when you knew, we all *knew* that you knew, that we knew,
you had spare ones, with the airline name written down the side,
in the *Luxury Goods* duty-free rip-off trolley,
thus you forcing the poor dear poet
to write in lipstick, on the back of a used sick bag.
You must understand that the poet had had
a marvellous inspiration upon take-off?
It could have been the greatest genius
of our lifetimes, lifetimes, lifetimes.
Please note that instead this was what she wrote
on that same short flight to Austria:

Dearest Sky Barmaid,
with your Halloween pumpkin slit for an inane smile,
this one is not for you – you sour-faced citrus –
but about you – you mottled mandarin-skinned reptile.
I demand, you bring me ten more vodkas,
as I scrawl these words
blurred and smeared with carroty sick seeping through.

I hope that you enjoy a miserable monotonous life
like a one-winged bird going in circles
with no real destination or purpose,
your cupreous skin like poor quality leather goods
from all those sunbeds and
your jowls sagging from all that hair-bun pinning,
stinking of cheap citric acid perfume,
your arsehole limp from aeroplane fibre-free foodstuff
and all those rough dry arse-rape searches
your're going to get at every landing.
I see you baby,
I see your peach painted talons clinging to an oxygen mask
whilst you lose that very pen up your arse
or to an insane suicidal madman
who uses it to write his demands on your face,
mistaking it for an orange Post-it note pad.
I hope that pen leaks all over your uniform
and dyes your right tit blue.
I hope you choke on rancid pilot sperm.

Bon voyage!
Seat 66A

A Letter to a Young Poet

HOTEL BUBROVNIK
ZAGREB, CROATIA

November 2001

Dear M-

I don't know where to begin...there are so many words running around my happy and tired mind that it is really quite difficult to make them form an orderly queue. I have heard such stories and been met with such a flow of conflict in my pre-conceptions of Bosnians and Croatians, of war and politics, of geography and 20th century world history. I am writing this in my hotel room awaiting a telephone radio interview to promote the FAK YU, the reason I am here, the FAK YU literature festival.

On my arrival in Zagreb airport I was met by two unlikely looking fellows, both hairy faced and smoking. They asked me if I came from London I said yes and got in their car. I was thinking I was being driven to some war-ravaged, crack-infested, whore-slave-trade basement as my mother had warned me, but alas and of course, I am delivered safely to Klub Gjuro and FAK and there I was met, so warmly, by Borivoj Radakovic, the organiser and a writer, who invited me here to read my poetry, we all call him Boro.

Boro chain-smoked, he smoked strong Croatian cigarettes, Opatija, continually. He had a flash of white hair and this deeply resonant voice with the strangest Mancunian-Northern lilt in his English. I was made immediately welcome with an onslaught of any and every drink I wanted. Boro drank beers, I drank vodka believing it was brewed here. Vodka, another pre-conception, the local beverage here is actually a type of brandy. However, I knew I was in good company, within twenty minutes I was taught how to tell people that their mothers should go do unspeakable things with dogs and I was instructed to repeat until perfected the word 'pitch-ka' which means cunt. As we chatted and drank and swore, photographers bulbs flashed and a national TV news team and crew lit the place up way too much. I slathered on lip-gloss and like to think I kept my end up.

Boro and I have many mutual friends and acquaintances especially from Filthy McNasty's. He mentioned writers that had come here before me: Ben Richards, Jackie Kay, Matt Thorn, Nicolas Blincoe, Julian Barnes and John Cooper Clarke who he could quote brilliantly – and therein I perhaps saw the source for his subtle Mancunian accent!

I was introduced to many writers, authors and publishers from Croatia, Bosnia and Serbia. I was surrounded literally and literally by people that love books, writing them as much as reading them, literary anarchists, word warriors, reading renegades, heroes and heroines plus an audience that loved them. This was the start of the reaffirmation of the whole trip, the sewing of the seeds of ideas that I now write to you, I have seen it M-, I feel renewed and my doubts have evaporated. Before I came here I was starting to believe that poetry and spoken word is a very unique skill merely for specialist audiences, for a chosen wholly literary few. That poetry is dead, or worse, that poetry is an old rowing boat with only one oar, going in circles, never moving anywhere. Poetry is the Titanic, and I could never be anything like the captain who shoots himself in the head. Or the silver-haired Victorian refusing to accept defeat, clutching her jewels, laying in her sodden bed, weeping as sea-water seeps through the porthole. I would rather jump and swim and take my chances with the sharks and the fire and ice.

I do not believe that poetry has to be difficult or locked. I believe the difference between here and home is reverence and respect. Let us not forget the difficulties with language barriers, cultural references and cultural sensitivities here, yet these audiences listened without explanations or compromises on my part. Indeed, here in Zagreb over 1000 people turned up three nights in a row and paid to hear, to listen and to support their writers, the poets, for it is us who knot the common thread of moment.

The only other time I have witnessed this support and belief among writers, making voices heard, was in January in East Timor. The poetry and music of the country and of the resistance fighters was cherished and the poems were learned and repeated in defiance of the state and government. In Timor they told me how people were imprisoned and killed for the singing of certain songs. I find myself thinking of apartheid and Africa, the tradition of story-telling and the passing-on of stories and poems, of grandmothers all over the world spinning yarns and I think of censorship and consider how grateful I am to even write this, that it may be read as freely as it is written. We still have FREE SPEECH and we can never under estimate this.

So, then perhaps it is true, maybe these hard times, war and poverty, breed a greater need and understanding of the importance of literature and poetry. Maybe during volatile times there is a heightened necessity to fight together as artists and writers, as the people turn to artists and authors for not just entertainment and satire but also a clear documentation of the present.

I wonder what we must do, what we must witness and live through, so we can execute this trend in cynical, stir up the apathy, this lack of conviction. What does it take to put razors and stones into the comfortable slippers of light-entertainment and mediocre drivel like Bridget Jones and other chick lit crap. I suppose I could suggest that Bridget Jones is important as it mirrors and documents the early 21st century trend in lethargic complacency and is living proof that all a publisher wants to publish is a book about a girl who is lost until she finds a 'good man'…The End? Really? Don't get me started…sorry…I know I'm ranting…again.

I am trying to write to you to urge you to keep writing and to always write. Never, never give up. From East Timor, to 9/11 to here, I am discovering people like us, people that do care about poetry, about documenting our times, sharing beautiful books, good writing and inspiring stories. I am writing to tell you of Croatia, of Zagreb and of these anarchists and renegades and provocative story-tellers and artists, these new-old-friends I have found.

That first day with Boro we had lunch. He met me at one o'clock and we were there drinking until it was dark and past five. We feasted on homemade breads, kulun – its a kind of dried spiced pork – and Livno cheese. And we drank clear pear brandies chased by Ozujsko Pivo beers. I grasped for some association with other cities, there were similarities with German sausage, Hungarian goulash and Austrian pancake soup.

74

There is Grappe. There is also a dish here which is very popular made of boiled cottage cheese. Boro smokes constantly and tells me stories of all the war and unrest, he talks of freedom and liberty, of the rise of communism and nazi fascists, of a willingness to speak out and he tells these stories with such spirit it is contagious. He makes me feel as though there is nothing more important than being a writer.

Boro and I walked arm in arm in the rain down the cobbled main street to the deaf and mute institute. He lent me his hat and I walked tall by his side. I watched Croatian stories being read and interpreted into sign language. It is alarming how much we can understand by the melody and feeling of a voice, without the tools of knowing the meaning, the bone and gristle, we still taste and chew the meat of the words, words are marrow.

I have been told that Salena means Saliva in Croatian, so my name Salena Saliva is like a double pool of spit here. I have been told that Zagreb is on the 16th Meridian line and is in alignment with Prague and Vienna. What else? Well if you want to picture it, many of the old buildings, the old Theatre for instance, are painted this deep dark banana yellow. I will always remember the sun shining through the late-Autumn leaves, there is a distinctive marriage of gold and amber against the bright wintry blue sky, it's truly beautiful.

We must come here together one day. I will post this now so you will have a real Croatian stamp for your collection. Ha ha! I know you don't collect stamps, but it's never too late to start. I will raise a glass to you and I promise to bring you home some of this most excellent Pear Brandy!

Keep the ink wet and keep it burning,
With all my love,
Saliva xxx

That Ordinary Day in Santa Cruz

I drop Emily off to work
at the needle exchange,
then head to the boardwalk,
my sign reads:
Buy A Poem – Feed A Poet

The pier is busy,
sea-lions bark whilst
tourists cameras click,
after an hour
I've made only one dollar.
Having sold one book cheap
because she looked like she'd like
actually read it.

I scrounge a roll-up
from a dread-locked jeweller.
He makes me an ankle chain,
of turquoise and black beads
and fastens it on for me.

I walk down Pacific
and stop in record-shops and bookstores,
they take a few books each,
and let me pin posters up
for a reading I hustled that night
in the Poet and Patriot pub.
It is owned by a Dublin man,
yesterday I ordered Guinness
and charmed him with a *hey James Bond,
you look just like Sean Connery…*

Back at the Needle Exchange,
the addicts hand in their used rigs.
I watch needles go into bio-hazard boxes,
fascinated, I'm like a child
examining seagulls feathers,
for blood on the tip.

I help Emily.
I hand out condoms
and bagged cottons,
got any 27's?
They ask her.
Need swabs?
She replies.
It's about harm reduction:
Fuck Safe – Shoot Clean.

I listen to wild boasts
of busts and bail,
shoplifting and jail,
septic wounds and collapsed veins.
Someone had tried to inject in the neck,
and it had gone
wrong.

The pub is packed,
as I do my reading
people buy me beers,
light my cigarettes and
the jug goes around,
soon spilling over
with more than enough
to get me East,
back to New York
and eventually
home.

That night,
I didn't want to leave California.
My heart was there
and this was home.
I knew every face in the bar.
I knew everybody and
I remember every kindness,
from that extraordinary day
in Santa Cruz.

Tribute to Cheryl B.

It's the red lipstick
I remember first
and how privately
I thought of you as my very own
Dorothy Parker.
Your sharp Manhattan wit
brutal honesty and
a heart that spilled and splashed
and silenced a room.

Your eyes were two black orchids
in smooth pale moonlight,
but your mouth was blood
scarlet and dark as the words
that hooked us
quick
smart.

Your writing always made me wish
people were more
kind.

So it goes like this…

We met in maybe 1995
maybe '96.
With Tim Wells, of course
Mr Wells connects us all,
the Heart of Darkness crew,
Rising and rising
you rose, you rose.

But who can remember that first meeting?
Was it at the Enterprise with Lyallsy?
Perhaps with Turnbull, Ivan and 'Cesca
Paul Birtill might have been there too…

It is for sure we would have gone to the Marathon for afters
for chips and beers and Johnny Cash and Jack and coke.
Back then when it was still OK to smoke fags indoors
and we would ride the milk float home at dawn.

Then late in 1998 and '99
there was dirty snow along the gutters of Bowery.
We read together at CBGB's, Steve Cannon's Tribes Gallery
Blue Stockings, the Telephone Bar and St Marks.
We demolished dozens of jugs of frozen margheritas
in a place with a name like Mexican Hat
with Aimee Bianca.

I remember skidding on icy Brooklyn sidewalks
snowball fights and high times
and sucking beer up in polysterene cups
at The Green Point Tavern.

Remember that stinking hot summer of 2001?
And that disastrous gig at the Cornelia Street Café?
You were right when you said,
poetry is full of mad people,
but that was the summer
the world went mad too
we witnessed 9/11
and things haven't been the same since.

The last time I saw you was 2007.
I was returning from a writing bender in Cornwall
I arrived in Waterloo in the nick of time
for us to read together with Adele Stripe and the gang.
You were a non-drinker by then
but you winked and said:
have a good time did you?

Now it's 2011
you have gone too young and
it's snowing in June and poets are still mad,
focussed on ambition and celebrity
instead of real guts and truth.

But you, Cheryl,
you were a pearl
and it feels like the world is running low on grit
its gonna be nothing but a clatter of empty oyster shells
without you, my friend.

It's Best Not to be Alone

This morning
my first reaction was,
not again.

My phone was ringing off the hook,
that was when I put on the TV
and saw Tavistock Square,
a smashed red bus,
bloodied victims,
shattered glass...

Not again.
It is July 7th 2005
and London is an ant hill under attack.
We are British and we keep calm and carry on.
We send messages to the ants at the back
to use the easier routes through town.
We are told to stay home, stay safe.

I walk to the corner of my road
to my local pub and the landlord Nick says
it's best not be alone at times like this.
Buying me a drink, Nick tells me
at times like this you need to be around people.

There was a sense of unity in the pub
Text messages all read:
Are you and yours OK?
We are counting blessings.
The romance of the old Blitz spirit
described by all our grandparents
glows like an old flame and we
pride ourselves on that.

There are some who shrug and spit,
we deserve it and they deserve it.
They are fucking idiots.

This is a beautiful world.
Nobody deserves it.
No-one deserves
bombs.

We all deserve
peace and
love.

Twat

If you'd like a poet
to write about you
be a twat.
And if you want a poem
written all about you
be a twat to a poet.

Because poets don't often
write about nice people
or people they love
until it's too late
and they are dead.

So if you want to be
immortalised in a poem
either be kind and die,
or be a twat.

And if you want to be
ranted about from stages
in literature festivals and
hear about yourself on BBC Radio 4,
be a twat.

And if you want to see
yourself in print
in the poetry section
and in arty magazines
and anthologies
be a twat.
And if you want
to have school children gasp
about your wickedness,
and students
shake their heads in disgust
at the protagonist in this poem,
that's you,
that's all about you,
you twat, then
be a twat.

That's right just like that
be a twat, you carry on
be yourself, be a twat,
just like that, be a twat
just like that, you twat.

It must make you feel
like being a twat
knowing that
you will live forever
and ever in library archives
and recorded for prosperity.

So be a twat
be the twat in this poem
if you like
this one is all about you,
you twat!

Hoorah!
A poem about me.
Hello!
I'm the twat
to which poem is referring.
Yes, it's really me,
pleased to meet you,
nice to put a name
to a face and a face to a name.

I'm not just any twat,
I am the twat,
the twat in the poem
I am THE Twat!

Or even worse I am me
I am the poet twat
that should just forget the twat.
I am the poet twat
that wrote this poem
about a twat,
twat poet, twat poet,
twat twat twat!

If the Heart is a Bell

For Gigi Giannuzzi

Tonight, I write for you Gigi
and it's not easy at all
to write of you in the past tense.
The last orders call,
time, gentlemen, please,
stop the clock, it's gone too fast,
so we write of the sound of your beginning
your first breath – not your last.

You once told me,
late one night,
you were born in Rome
at the strike of midnight,
and that every bell rang out
as you opened your eyes to see first light,

every cathedral and church bell swinging
chiming, ringing, clanging, singing,
a cacophony of pealing bells beating,
sonorous and resound,
intensified, glorified,
reverberating and profound.

It's odd the things we remember.
And it doesn't matter if this was true,
if all the bells in all the world
were merrily ringing out for you.
But it's the passion of you I hear,
we won't let that music disappear.
It's the people we love, we met through you,
the Trolley family, far and near and, dear.

Gigi,
tonight I write for you,
how quiet this winter seems to be,
but if I listen carefully I hear summertime.
Your boisterous laughter, restlessly.
I see you beam your generous grin,
a smile that skids across your cheeks and chin,
lips stained blue with wine, Gigi,
raucous banter, to get a word in...

And you're wearing your Venetian slippers,
your sarong or your velvet suit of red,
Redchurch Street, the roaring chorus of artists,
a clatter of chatter, dusk 'til dawn 'til bed.

Most of all though it's this –
your birth in Rome and in July,
I imagine the bells chiming for Gigi,
Italian moonlight, stars, a midnight sky.

And it's the sound of you I'm listening for.
A boom, a bark, a buzz of energy,
and how you believed in us all.
Believed in this, believed in me.

If a heart is a bell
then mine is swinging.
We're all chiming, ringing,
clanging, singing,
I hear a symphony of one love.
Hearts gathered, beating,
sonorous and resound,
intensified, glorified,
reverberating and profound.

Housewives in Birmingham

It is exactly three o'clock in the afternoon. I am still in my pyjama bottoms, a pink Barbie T-shirt and I look like shit. Outside there is a whitish sky, a dull wallpaper that never changes or moves. My kitchen smells of burnt toast – you see I cannot even get that right.

My agent is using the hard-love tactic, telling me I ought to look at the bright side, at least I *have* a book deal. I listen and remind myself this is all teaching me patience and that all of this is a test of my endurance; truth is, phone calls with my agent remind me of speaking to the Samaritans.

Every time I submit another edit to the publishers, a chopped-up headless draft comes back six months later, when I have lost momentum. I return to the battlefield to find blood-red snipers in the margins. My book is a soldier in a body bag which I struggle to recognise with all the bullet holes.

Loathing myself, I begin to say something like, "I feel like I am at the bottom of some pecking order…" *Well you are,* my agent reminds me, *I am afraid to tell you this, but you are. Housewives in Birmingham don't know your work or who you are, and that's who we have to sell you to and that is going to take time.* I tell my agent he is right, we say goodbye and hang up. I smoke and stare into space and think about housewives in Birmingham. I picture them masturbating on washing machines during daytime TV.

Housewives in Birmingham
going to sex swinger parties.
Housewives in Birmingham
weeping over books by Katie Price and Jade Goody.
Housewives in Birmingham
on Ibiza hen nights scratching each other raw.
Housewives in Birmingham
tearing into each other on reality television.
Housewives in Birmingham
making their husbands wear black plastic gimp suits.
Housewives in Birmingham
scoffing curries in the rain at the end of the night.

I am in a Tesco supermarket in Birmingham –
my book is in her trolley next to frozen potato shaped products and
spaghetti letters.

I am in an Ann Summers in Birmingham –
my book is in her bag next to vibrating anal beads and fluffy pink
hand cuffs.

I am in an Oxfam in Birmingham –
my book is in her hand. Someone has pencilled £1 on my book cover.

I dare not leave the house, the seagulls are taunting me: When is your
book out? When is your book out? Believe me you'll know about it,
you'll know about it. Even if you are a housewife in Birmingham, I'll
make sure you bloody know about it.

My friends tell me all the great books were difficult and I repeat this to
myself, like I reckon I am Carver or Bukowski. This bravado doesn't
last and words like outsider and edgy have began to echo with failure.

I go into the bathroom and strip off, I mean to take the bath drawn
hours ago. But it's still too hot, too full to pull out the plug to pour
some away – you see I cannot even get that right.

I climb back into bed and feel sick. Its already getting dark outside.
There are days like these more often than not, and I fail to see the
point in any of it.

I write this poem for you, for the Housewives in Birmingham.
It is all about Led Zepplin and the black country
and worshipping Satan.

I reach for my mobile phone and switch it off, pull the landline plug
out of the wall, put a pillow over my face – it's nice and dark there.

I'm not stupid, I know things could be worse, I could always be dead
or I could wake up and be a housewife in Birmingham.

Swan

We live on a river in the country,
we talk gently and listen easy,
we lost our smoky bark and city hiss.
You'll play me the guitar, whilst I knead dough.
I make enough bread to feed the ten sons
we never made time to have.
You get under my feet when I ask you to
whisk the milk. Stir the gravy. Mind the oven.
We never agree about the temperature, maps and train time tables.

You hold the pegs whilst I hang the washing,
on the line hung between low-hanging crab-apple trees.
Our ramshackle garden is overgrown
and there are spiders in the lavender.
The radio plays the shipping forecast.
It's getting cold. Cold enough to snow.
No. Not yet.

A skein of geese flock overhead,
but you and me, we never migrated apart.
Together we become weathered
and soft as old cotton and as yellow as warm butter.
We keep chickens and ducks that rarely lay eggs,
an obnoxious mallard nests like royalty
in an armchair in the parlour.

Of course we brew our own beer
and we grow grass and tomatoes in the conservatory.
Laughter. Yes, we still laugh,
the lines are etched around our failing eyes.
Foam and lathered we bathe together too,
and play cards and drink rum and dare each other to
skinny-dip in the lake by the weeping willow when the moon is high.

Books are precariously balanced on slanting shelves
and guitars are in varying states of loving repair.
Boxes of dusty poetry and newspaper cuttings clutter the stairs.
And the piano has a few keys missing,
like teeth and the scissors and your spectacles –
they are on your head, you nincompoop!

We've collected empty Marmite jars for no reason,
no reason at all.

We get tired, we go to bed, have sex in the afternoon.
Snow flutters like feathers past the frosty winter windows.
Face to face, we lie on the cool side of the pillow,
wrapped in each other's arms like two monkeys.
My fingers play with the silver hair at your temples,
you stroke my face and I breathe slowly.
Jigsaw pieces.
We always did fit nicely.

You call me in my dreams at night.
I've felt your plush wings
spread wide, enveloping me.
You and me, we will have all this and more,
we will have all this in time.
I have known you all my life.
We will find each other
one day,
my swan.

Limp Expectations

I'm gonna go limp on my high expectations
and dream small dreams.
Gonna go limp on my high expectations
and dream tiny tidy dreams.
Stop going over the top, reel myself in,
teach myself to stop before I even begin.
Gonna stop getting carried away
with wanting my own way, with having a say,
dream small dreams, have no expectations,
no more daydreaming my days away.
You could write my tiny tidy dreams
on a grain of rice, on a piece of ice,
on an ant's eyelash, on an amoeba's moustache.
I know everything that happens happens for a reason.
That's a good reason to stop anything happening, stop,
stop this dream, I'm getting off.
I'm gonna have low expectations,
gonna have no expectations, so low,
no expectations, so low, gonna go solo, so low.
I'm gonna dream small and achievable dreams.
I wanted some milk, I went to the shop,
I bought a pint of milk, my dream is achieved.
Gonna go limp on my high-faluting expectations
and dream miniscule dreams.
Gonna take small steps, tiny steps,
I'm gonna wanna take steps backwards,
two steps backwards and no steps forwards.
In fact, why don't you come sit on the end of my bed
and tell me what to dream at night?
Sit on the end of my bed and tell me what to dream
just so I know I am getting my dreams small enough,
tiny and tidy enough, right.
I'm gonna stop assuming
people have the same priorities as me,

gonna stop pushing and pulling the forces around me,
stop expecting people to have the same energy as me,
stop expecting people to have any, any energy.
I will not resent this – but go with the flow.
I am going to go so slow and go with the flow, solo, so low.
I will not swim against the tide
or upset the apple-cart or make any waves.
I'm just here for the ride, so please take a photo,
tag it on my Facebook.
This is a picture of me giving up and letting go.
I had a dream, past tense had, had a dream,
but it was so small and undernourished,
barely worth mentioning.
I'm no longer frozen by fear of success.
I'm no longer frozen by fear of failure.
I expect neither, success nor failure,
I know it's the taking part that counts
and I am fine with that.
Gonna weaken my grip on wanting anything,
stop holding onto my high expectations,
my fancy ideas, fancy-shmancy dream,
my great expectation
that we could do better,
that we could pull in the same direction,
that we could give more,
that we could all do more,
that we could be more.
I challenge nothing and I challenge nobody.
I accept you all and I accept all of this, all of you.
Gonna take life as it comes and accept my hand.
Gonna take myself home and lock my box,
lock myself in a box inside another box,
and in the glow of no hope of no change
I will perhaps one day forgive myself
for giving up.

I Want Love

I want love.
I want love all over me.
I want to be on top of love.
I want love to surround me.
I want to be inside love.
I want love to be inside me.
I want to be consumed with love, by love.
I want to be in love.
I want to love so hard that I go home early from the pub.
I want to quit drinking and smoking for love.
I want to quit crossing the road when it's busy.
I want to quit putting salt on unsalted butter because
I want to live so long so I can love this love as long as I can.
I want a house built with love.
I want a garden blooming with love and
I want beautiful children with all the love I have.
I want children made of love, with love,
for love and in love's name.
I want to have so much love I reek of it,
it stains my clothes and fingers.
I want love to leak from me.
I want love to knot in my hair.
I want love under my nails.
I want to drink love.
I want to eat love.
I want to open the fridge and find love.
I want to find love in the oven.

I want to sleep with love and
I want to wake up with love.
I want to hear love on the radio.
I want to sing the songs of love.
I want to write the words of love.
I want to bathe love.
I want to wash love's clothes.
I want to clip love's toenails.
I want to make love soup and love pie.
I want to make love make love.
I want to care for love in love's sickbed.
I want to find the bail to get love out of jail.
I want to go to prison for love.
I want to die for love.
I want to kill for love.
I want to throw myself off a cliff for love.
I want love to be like a cancer.
I want to be terminally ill with love.
I want to be riddled incurably with love.
I want to fuck love in the arse.
I want to fuck love up.
I want to fuck love over.
I want to fuck love, fuck love.
I want to but I can't.

The End of the World as We Knew it

The Puerto Rican coke dealer and I were an unlikely team.
We were characters in a jail escape movie
hiding out and shackled together
looking for a hacksaw
but not wanting to be separated after all...

I sat on the window ledge of a cheap hotel room.
I was small and damp from the shower.
I drank and watched black smoke guff thickly
into Manhattan's postcard sunset skyline.

New York stank of barbecues and worse.
Nobody ever talks about the stench
or the frenzy to claim a piece,
those crazy hoax victims on American TV
or the lost shoes in the gutters and the dread-filled silence
and how every bar spilled with gallows humour and irony.

How we all drank like there was no tomorrow,
because for all we knew there was no tomorrow.

I didn't eat or sleep for days,
I bar hopped and pub crawled
collecting conspiracies and bad taste jokes.
But Cokey, he looked after me.
He bought me a toothbrush and
an omelette I pushed about my plate
devouring vodka and Marlboro instead.
Paranoid. Frightened. Wired.

Word spread there were
concentration camps at JFK airport.
And that this was it,
the end of the world as we knew it.

The greatest bar on earth was in flame.
This was the last party ever
and the biggest drink of my life
and I was going out of my mind
holed up in some sleazy Brooklyn motel
with a dark-eyed stranger who made sense,
who made more sense than the censored TV
and the pool table jokers.

We made out like it was the last fuck on the planet.
He told me I was beautiful.
Of course he did.
I remember his brown arms around me,
his accent like rum and sugar cane
and I felt safe there.

I thought, this is how I die then,
this is the way to go,
nice and numb and easy.

I watched the sun set in the black sky
and I told him
there is only one thing we can count on –
that the sun will set there,
here, be unique, each and every day
and we both believed that little.

Weeks later,
I made it home to London.
I was shocked and angry
bar hopping and pub crawling
and some people, they kept saying
that America deserved it.

No.
No life deserves this.
No one deserves this.
Our lives, this life,
Us. This our beautiful life,
our living and breathing life,
no life deserves war and flames.
I wish people used indifference
when purchasing cereals
instead of when passing blame and death.

Maybe, there is only one thing you can truly count on –
that the sun will set and be there, each and every day,
even when we are all fried,
even when we are all dead and done and
dusted.

At Night They Made God

Last night there was
a vibration through the house,
the walls and windows rattled,
there was a measured banging rhythm
without apology or regret,
I wanted to go upstairs
to watch and applaud.

It sounded like
they were making a king,
intentionally,
at least I hoped they were.
That kid would be rare,
a lover, a fighter,
a revolutionary.

There was love in the room upstairs
and I decided I was witnessing
the making of a great leader,
a legend or a great writer,
a composer or a genius painter,
the one to cure cancer,
solve world poverty
and stop all this war.

Convinced of all of this
I rolled over
and went back to sleep
alone.

Relieved it wasn't my job
to watch him teething,
feed him his greens
and protect him
from cynics
and rapists.

The alive and the living are coming,
they come alive in the night.
The alive and the living are coming

and coming and coming
they come and come again
they come alive in the night.

The humans are making God
whilst the Devil makes sleep
for idle dreamers.

Peppermint Whiskey

She rebooted herself
to the original factory setting
to the way I was made inside.
She's pressing restart on my heart
normal service to be resumed
once we reset the soul
and wipe the corrupted files
from this hard drive

She's been snow blind
with poor excuses
disrupting
any present tense,
it's all white noise and fuzz,
her ear
is pressed up to the past
love
like a toothbrush glass
drained of whiskey
and pushed against the beige hotel wall
of a dream I once broke.

She gets over it
as soon as she starts hearing
the same shit

that made her feel
so small and hard
because she was feeling
something,
anything
in the first place.

There's no more
space
in the memory
just a ringing in the senses
the sting of a slap
and a burn in the throat.

And
now I recognise
something
the wallpaper stained
with old sweat
the odour of fear
the headboard daubed
with greasy grabbing handprints
from the last hairy asshole
who left a plaster
in the plughole
and didn't flush
the chain.

Outside the moon is full and black
and blood is a constant
and vivid reminder
that we are all animals
whores and magicians.

I recognise my own cries
squeals and grunts
from the room next door
the window flashes with neon
cheap, cheap, cheap!
Used car tyres!
Taxi!

The computer crashed
the program is outdated
but we've all been here before
swinging without
a tree to cling to.

Back then when
I had better teeth
and used the toothbrush glass
to swill Listerine
instead of Jameson,

back then when
computers were for games
and mobile phones
came with a suitcase,

back then when
thighs were bruised
by bony hips –
and we all didn't expect
to live this long.

The glass swilled
with peppermint and whiskey
pressed against the walls
of the past
love,

the wet circle
leaves a mark
for the future
on bad wallpaper.
We will delete that
screen saver.

But she keeps listening
for what I want to hear
and she doesn't believe this
love
and I don't believe
my own ears.

This is How it Goes

She says –
out of the blue
her friend calls by.
Weeks can pass
between visits,
he comes and
he goes.

There is no obligation,
no neediness,
and when he is there,
they get along fine.

She boasts that he has
exquisite manners
in the bedroom.
He's a real gentleman.

They eat together in the café
and their lips glisten
with all-day breakfast
running down their chins.
They talk with their mouths full.

They make quite the handsome pair.
You overhear them debating matters of the heart
and Raymond Carver.
At night he often reads to her –
something beautiful by Chekhov.

To pay his rent
he goes to plump hotels,
and fucks MPs in the arse.

He dominates middle-aged men
with whips and chains
in crisp white sheets
for crisp pink notes.

She notices
his lean and long body
is wounded, bitten and bruised
and she says nothing.

He is a dozen years
younger than her,
but she's been around
long enough to know
this is as good as it goes –
and this is as good as it comes.

They don't label it.
If they gave it a name
like love,
promises and rules
would get broken
and shit –
one night
the condom split.

They laughed and named
the potential child.
She tried on his surname
as they walked hand in hand
to the chemist.
She sings, *Roxanne*
you don't have to
put on the red light.

Of course,
they feared the worst
but he was still grinning
as she started worrying how
on earth she'd look after
all three of them.

When I meet her
outside the pub,
she shoves
a morning-after pill
down her throat,
washes it down
with wine and soda.

He says goodbye
and cycles away
to a job in one of
Piccadilly's fattest hotels.

She waves and hopes
she won't get sick
or get a migraine
and puke up the pill.
At least that's
just one of her hopes
and worries.

Sometimes,
she says,
sometimes,
this is how it goes,
and sometimes,
she says, sometimes this
is as good as it comes.

Milk Thistle and Juniper

Then we took the child with hair like the milkman
down past the cow sheds, through the milky dusk light,
auburn rust on our bikes, we hid by the roadside,
broken glass where the juniper gin jar smashed drunk.

Then we took the child with hair like the milkman
when primroses yellowed, snowdrops edged brown with time.
Budding trees bowed to canopy the green ivy like
the velvet waistcoat worn by the doctor from Galway and never to tell.

Then we took the child with hair like the milkman,
dead weight was the bitter secret, curdled like curds and whey
it sticks in the throat like a dry hoarse clotted-cream cough
that bathtub gin and a kick from the horse couldn't cure.

Then we took the child with hair like the milkman
as a train whistled steaming past up through the clearing,
the cowslips danced with milk thistle, sister lay on the blanket,
prayed to merciful Mary above the scuds of bloated soured clouds.

Then we took the child with hair like the milkman
before she would show and so no one would know,
before waters broke streaming and screaming the dawn
with coat-hanger tangled and the salt to the slugs
that slid past in the undergrowth, never to tell.

Then we took the child with hair like the milkman
out. Wrapped in the blanket and wet with soft bones dead.
Buried with feathers of crows, a poppy like red flows,
bloodied the muddied moss of the pebbled brook stream.

Then we took the child with hair like the milkman,
our knotted stained petticoats,
our bloody soiled dress-skirts,
washed our shame in naked silence,
dirty and shadowed with tears,
and the milkman knew nothing and so never to tell.

We took the child with hair like the milkman
out. Buried with blood-sodden clothes,
feathers of crows, and a poppy like red flows,
the watery grave, the brook babbles the secret
and we swore like the salt to the slugs never to tell.

When I Heard the Man

For Gil Scott-Heron & Martin Luther King

When I heard the man
I fell into sky blue
of lyrics that were true
with courage and faith
and that wicked wolf
lit the pathway of doubt
the world went too fast
but one day won't last
long enough to recall
it's about how you get up
and not how you fall
it's how we get up
and not how we fall.

When I heard the man
I fell into sky blue,
too true, my mind wandered back
across fields of then-then
rivers of thereafter
now where do you go
and what can you do
but believe in yourself, but
you sometimes forget
hold on, whoa, it's not your turn yet
and what made you so sure
you'd get a turn fair and square?
stick with the love
hate's too great a burden to bear
stick with the love, hate's too great a burden to bear
know where are you going
stop standing there
you're running, running
but you ain't going nowhere
it's like wetting the whistle
but making no tune
Winter in America
Whitey on the Moon

I once met the man
and I shook his hand
fell into sky blue
his smile was true

and that wicked wolf
knew the way through them woods
through the bracken and twists
dark and the bottle
Storm Music flowed from his wrists
whilst the wind blew the hands
of the clocks round too fast
a whole day won't last
so don't cling onto your beer
we have nothing to fear
but a fear of the fear
nothing to fear
but fear itself, dear.

When I heard the man
I fell into a truth
a lie cannot live
not a lie in a word
a riot is the language
of the unheard
a riot is the language of the unheard
stealing Nike trainers
and more angers stirred
faith is taking the first step
when you don't see the whole staircase
got some justice for Lawrence
and next Smiley's case?

I heard *Pieces of a Man*
I fell into the blue
and that wicked wolf
left the door ajar
moonlight seeped through
onto a world spinning too fast
but a whole day don't last
long enough to pick up old taxes
big trees and small axes
the forest washes bright
fall into the blue, fall into the light.
In the end we remember
not the words of our enemies
but the silence of friends

occupy your space
do your being, be your action
live love, love life, alive to the ends
Lady Day and John Coltrane
bloody London pours
with bloody lovely London rain
ain't nothing but a B movie
and the weather's awry
I'm gonna take me a piece of sunshine
and paint it all over my sky.

Where I Live

Where I live
there is no bathroom
so we strip wash
in a plastic baby bath in front of the wood burner.

Where I live
there is no running hot water
so we boil pots
and I wash my hair in the sink.

Where I live
there is no toilet seat
or lock on the door
so I balance there and hope.

Where I live
there are no stairs
so I so precariously
climb a ladder to go to bed at night.

Where I live
the roof leaks but I don't mind
it waters the plants
and washes the dusty floorboards.

Where I live
there are mice
but people say that where there are mice
there cannot be rats.

This morning the landlords cut off the water
I had to wash my face
and clean my teeth
in the pint of water by the bedside.
I don't live
where I live
on purpose.

I'm a girl
not an art installation.
I do not aspire to be
a starving poet cliché

And
if I had the four thousand pounds
I owe the landlords
I obviously wouldn't live

Where I live.

Wyoming Road Kill

We passed River Bighorn
and Custer's last stand.
The sky was on fire ahead of us
and behind us we left a trail
kicked up dust and grit
as we crossed the border
into Montana,
rabbit fur on the fender.

She made me think
Of Mice and Men,
slow, sloth, mechanical,
medication slurring
her braying laments
for Bugs Bunny,

and the bugs smeared,
splat, across the windshield.
I concentrated on the road
and the wine bottle
between my knees
nearly all done.

Montana Mike.
I took off his glasses and baseball cap,
cut his hair and shaved him,
in the shower he scrubbed up good
all firm and wet against
the slippery tiled bathroom wall.
Fucking like mountain rabbits.
Eyes wide, strong back legs,
freckled forearms,
I remember that much
and that little.

And the heat
and the mountain air
and the stars
all went to her head.
I could say
it was in an act of self-defence.
It was gutting –
like she took a knife and tore
slashed from throat to belly.
I just wanted to pet him.

I became an accomplice whilst sleeping,
you could say it was a drunk misunderstanding,
and a bone just needs to be buried.

White morning light sobered,
we drive with the snow-capped mountains behind us,
ahead of us repulsion, hysterical excuses,
laughing: like I just wanted to pet him.
State line, we stop for eggs and biscuits.
She picks up her plate,
puckers and sucks up three yolks.

I gag, cramped up
into the stained, chequer restroom
A condom dislodges,
birthed into the toilet bowl.

Rabbit fur on the fender.
Should have kept the foot.

Have a Nice Day

In the Poughkeepsie Café
I order –
Please may I have
a cheese and salad sandwich?
The waitress looks blank
and says excuse me?
May I have a cheese and salad sandwich?
Oh, she says,
You want a what with cheese?
Salad? With cheese?
I am delirious
with exhaustion and hunger.
I am speaking in tongues,
seeing snakes and apparitions.
Please may I have a cheese and salad sandwich?
Do you want that grilled?
No, cold salad with mayo,
you know, tomatoes maybe,
lettuce, onions and cucumber.
She cheers.
Oh, we have mayo and we have onions.
She writes onions then
scribbles it out.
I try again.
Cold cheese and cold salad
sandwiched between two slices of cold bread.
Not that bit but that bit.
I point at a picture on the menu.
I say like burger but no burger.
Grilled cheese?
No, a not-cooked cheese and raw cold fresh salad sandwich please?
Not cooked? You mean like cooked rare right?
So you want home-fries with that?
I give up and ask for a beer,
the universal language.
It arrives just how I like it
on an empty stomach,
cold and un-grilled.

A Shot of Gasoline

I interviewed
my friend
Peter yesterday
for the BBC.

You can tell
how famous
Peter is now,
when he
bowled in
smoking,
nobody told him
to put it out and
Peter likes
to set fire to his head.

Everybody was
so like cool with it,
the producer
twitched nervously
trying to act comfortable
whilst Peter glowed.

I imagined them all
dining out on it,
supper at Claridge's,
with a mouthful
of roast woodcock,
they'll say
they met the beautiful boy,
they'll say
that he set his head on fire
and that they were
so like cool with it,
they even gave him
matches to play with,
they will mention
Icarus.

As he sets fire
to his head he cries and
they applaud
like it's the chorus,
not waving
but drowning,
no smoke
without fire.

It is capnolagnia
and pyromania
and the flames are
so pretty and gold.
It is rock and roll
to have scars and
to be in the process
of cooking your head.

But if I were to set my head alight
the BBC bosses
would waggle a finger
and tell me not to swear,
they'd send me outside
to set fire to my head
in the gutter quietly.

In the green room
Peter shows me
a library book by Genet.
I read his pencilled underlining
<u>the only truly significant relationship
is that of man with himself.</u>

I watch as
he plays guitar
alighting the room,
and there is that
heady smell
of burning flesh.
I am fighting
a terrible urge
to wrap a fireproof
blanket around him,
to rub butter on burns,
but instead I act
so like cool with it,
my only significant relationship
is my next shot of gasoline
with a petrol chaser.

I tremble and
eye the hose
wondering
if I should call 999
or if it's too
late.

The Heartland

In response to BBC Radio Festival debate, 'What's wrong with radio?'

It's been nearly twenty years since I first held a mic,
put it to my lips and said what I like
and in twenty years I bore witness to the evolution,
a literary explosion, the publishing revolution.
But the revolution will not be televised,
slipped between art and comedy and demoralised.
Poetry can't believe it's not butter as it's margarine-a-lised,
rinsed and bleached and sanitised

It's not what's wrong with radio
but surely what is write, right?
It seems far too scripted
and far too polite
because at festivals I see
it's the poets who stay up all night
and there is a rise in literary salons
where words kick and bite.

There is a heartland
in between the rap dream,
the coming of age teen and
the rock and roll scene and
the Booker prize winner
in the back of a limousine and
the struggling poet
writing in blood,
drinking ink and gasoline,
know what I mean?

The revolution will not be televised
but it's resonating on Resonance,
podcast and Twitterbooked.
The revolution will not be televised.
It's there on my iTunes
underground and overlooked,
the written word spoken,
delivered with intention,
even when it's not mainstream
or in The Times mentions.

Actions speak louder than words.
The pen is mightier than the clean page.
There is this heartland of undiscovered writing
between the outsider and the Hay-on-Wye stage

What is required, I feel,
is a literary John Peel
to open the gates and let in some light
because this revolution should be sung from the rooftops
and that's what's right with radio, right?
Write, right, write, right...
write, write, right.

Cloudbursting

He takes me
to his car
to seek shelter
from the hurricane.

Driving black rain
hammers metal
and batters the
steamed-up windscreen.

We meet
over the gear stick
his thumb inside me and
I lose myself in his mouth.

With the front seats
jammed flat
the heat and the music
on full blast

we strip
damp denim
twists around
my blue cowboy boots
the vehicle is
the rocking motion
of ships wrecked at sea
banging wild winds
and fucking.

Trees are bent double
with torrential downpour
inside the car pours
with sweat and
condensation,
I bite his lip
as we come and
then go again.

And we don't notice
the shanty town of
plastic tents fly past,

the storm blow over
the cream of daylight
like a split
milk bottle

or the morning dew
the haze of
distant fields
and hay bales.

I take his number
then stumble back
through the aftermath –
a festival camp site of
broken muddy things
and lost people.

He took me to his car
to seek shelter
from the
hurricane.

Hank is Alive and Well

If I approach his table
he'll pretend he doesn't understand me.
It's highly likely he refuses
to speak English anymore
or sign autographs –
I really should factor in
he may hate poetry
and poets recognising him.

But he looks well,
he looks bright
with the other old boys
playing dominoes
all gutsy and strong and silent,
he drinks plenty of beer,
chain smokes cigarettes,
he stands out with
that defiant air of bravado
a cocksure arrogance
like I bet he has a good one
swinging and throbbing
in his brown baggy pants.

I am drawn to the mole on his cheek
bushy knotted eyebrows
his creased forehead
the grey, greasy hair
and that pot belly in a sports shirt
is a sure give away.

I order a bottle of wine,
my Spanish is terrible,
the English laugh
at my pronunciation,
the make of the wine is
bocadero or bocadillo
but I just ordered
a bottle of sandwiches.

But it is then
after the second bottle is done
I decide it is in fact him!
He is the spit of the
black and white photo
from the cover of
ham on rye
post office
or factotum
I forget which but
I sit on my hands
fighting a raging
compulsion
to go sit on his lap
to play with the hairs
sprouting out of his purple ears.
I want to tweak
his purple bulbous nose.

Any minute now
I will call out the names
Charles? Hank? Chinaski?
and if he looks up
if he smiles at me
even once
I'm gonna get up
walk over there
cup my hands
about his big head
and kiss his
lovely craggy
face.

Imagine if You had to Lick it!

I have been doing this my whole life.
When I am hungover on a tube train or a bus
I stare at the most stomach turning churning things
and this voice inside my head says
IMAGINE IF YOU HAD TO LICK IT
that man's shiny bald patch with scabby dandruff
IMAGINE IF YOU HAD TO LICK IT
three-day-old vomit gone hard on the pavement
IMAGINE IF YOU HAD TO LICK IT
the zit on the girl's chin opposite
IMAGINE IF YOU HAD TO LICK IT
the tip of that man's finger firmly rooted up his left nostril
IMAGINE IF YOU HAD TO LICK IT
that runny old dog shit
IMAGINE IF YOU HAD TO LICK IT
that drunk man's piss in that doorway
IMAGINE IF YOU HAD TO LICK IT
those old Chinese takeaway noodles like maggots in the gutter by
the bin
IMAGINE IF YOU HAD TO LICK IT
lick it like you mean to clean it
IMAGINE IF YOU HAD TO LICK IT
lick it like you really mean it
IMAGINE
and I don't mean the tip but with the very back of your tongue
like the place that makes you retch if you touch it with a toothbrush
IMAGINE
all the people!
Imagine all the people…
licking them! all of them! licking them! all of them!
IMAGINE IF YOU HAD TO LICK IT
that pigeon's stumped foot
IMAGINE IF YOU HAD TO LICK IT
that tramp's cock!
I M A G I N E
I have been doing this all my life.
I find myself staring at the ugly and rotten
the rancid putrid essence
until I gag and I am forced to look away,
it makes the journey go faster
and it gives me something
else to be nauseous about…

Papillion Auschwitz

I spent seven days
pulling the wings off butterflies
for Damien Hirst,
she said.
All of us had to wear masks and gloves
because the butterflies were toxic.

They froze the butterflies,
she said.
They had to be frozen for two weeks.
They were farmed and gassed.
There was a fridge freezer
filled with fifty butterflies per bag.
You had to use tweezers to gently pull the wings off.

Does he have a concentration camp for caterpillars?
I asked.
Probably,
she replied.

But they are amazing, you know,
the butterflies look like a kaleidoscope
when you glue them onto a canvas in a pattern.

If I was a butterfly
I would call him Adolf Hirst.
If I was a caterpillar
I would like to be called Anne Butterfrank.

Are they expensive? I asked.
I don't know, she said,
but Sienna Miller bought one.

Frère Dearheart, Frère Dearheart, Dormez Vous?

That first night in Paris
we cannot sleep,
we wake every half hour
cold and uncomfortable

in a strange dark room,
a foreign bed in a new city
shivering and disgruntled
feet poking out from the covers.

We huff and pant,
toss and turn,
cough and tug
the sheets.

We elbow and shove
each other
like Laurel and Hardy
without slapstick laughs.

Dearheart stands naked and
smokes into the freezing icy
January night air,
he looks so serious,
smoking out of the open window
over his Paris.
Are you all right?

The little walrus snorts.
It's my birthday,
I am starving,
I only ate
six fucking snails!

I beat him with pillows
and yell at him to fight back,
we bounce on the bed,
he is foetal and laughing.

We talk about going out
to find adventure
in an oyster and
champagne bar.

It is 5am, it's Paris,
it's your birthday,
I say,
but oysters are no more
filling than snails!

We're excited
like it's Christmas Eve
and when the sun rises
we'll have all that Paris

all the champagne
and all the oysters we want
and we'll walk our tortoises
in the gardens of Notre Dame.

Viva Las Vegas

Makes me feel like a prostitute,
a cheap trick the way we got drunk so fast
and got a room on Las Vegas Boulevard,
the way you left your shorts
like you were leaving in such a hurry
whilst you thought I was sleeping.

I'm pleased you left your cigarettes
as I have no money and I really
want to smoke.
The room sweaty with the night before,
I look at a stain on the ceiling
dark like blood and coffee,
there's a dusty smell,
stale tobacco, socks and damp.

It feels cheap the way I've been stranded
in that Nevada slimy hotel,
left in the mess of tangled sheets,
used condoms,
the bathroom floor
strewn with towels,
some sticky remains
of Long Island iced tea.

It's a murder scene,
fingerprints all over me to be dusted,
evidence against me in a court of law,
baby, I'm going down.

I splash water at my face,
open the nylon curtains
to see the white heat rising and
the ghastly back of a concrete nothing.
I slowly drag last night's clothes
onto my used dried-sperm carcass.

I feel like a hooker
whose pimp robbed the cash,
sure we had a real good time
and maybe deep down and inside
I am a bit trashy.

Somebody wrote:
most women are mothers or whores
but all women are probably both.
Well, I feel like a whore's motherfucker
and the mother of all crack-whores.

Dehydrated,
sand for blood in my veins
mixing with alcohol
crystallised sugar
I'm sick as hell
and paranoid
that you may have left
without paying the bill.

I creep up to the desk to hand in the keys.
The woman snarls – *Name?*
I try to remember the hilarity
of the fake one you made up.

David... David... Smith?
I got a David... but it's not Smith.
Her lips pucker and pout,
she looks at me expectantly and says, *State?*
Yes I am!
I think,
leave me alone, you shrew.
I hedge a guess at
Chicago?
What did she expect?
Was I to know his blood type and car registration too?
C'mon lady,
I am a cheap drunk poet.
This is Vegas
and you have got to be kidding.

My Side of the Bar

I'm on my side of the bar
taking money in exchange
for glasses of forgetting
pints of could care less
shots of celebration.

She beams
with recognition.
Aren't you that poet?
I give an awkward nod
turn to face the ping
of the register.

She asks,
What are you doing?
Working here?
I explain
I live opposite,
that I do the odd
shift in my local
to keep the devil
from the wolves
at the door.

I don't remember her
or a gig we did once.
She smiles nasty
like she's discovered
my secret double life,
like, look how the
mighty have fallen.

Now, I wonder why I am
explaining myself,
more than why
I am on my side
of the bar.

Ribs

When I am dead
and I am a skeleton
I will be fascinating.
Deep sea researchers
will discover my bones
in the belly of a sunk ship,
a shipwreck once bound for China,
preserved by salt water,
coated in a blanket of algae.
I will be placed in a special box
marked 'fragile – handle with care'
and helicoptered to a laboratory
in Switzerland and kept
at a special frozen temperature
so I don't turn to mulch.
They'll make a film
about the clever find
for the History Channel.
The think tank will wear white coats,
plastic gloves and masks
so they don't breathe on me,
then a bearded young professor
with glasses, big hands
and a sexy deep voice
will poke my barnacled sockets
with a pointy stick.
Examining my skull,
he will say they have discovered
a wealthy lady of importance
and fine social standing,
just because of my two gold teeth.
He'll stroke his chin thoughtfully then say
look closely, see here, she lost a front tooth,
which is very, very interesting
because it could only have happened
when she was mashed at a festival in Ireland
and she fell down a well in Cork
with a pint of whiskey in each hand,
what a gal, she didn't spill a single drop!
Then with that, he'll get on the table
and lick my ribs out.

He Has the Same Dream

He has the same dream every night.
Betty Boop would be twenty inches tall
dancing and singing on his hairy belly
like an exotic lap dancer
she would pole dance
around his six-inch erection,
shoo boo bee boop she'd sing
shoobie doobie boobie doo
then she'd cover his member
in tiny titillating kisses
with her tiny titillating mouth.
Every morning he wakes up
next to his seventeen-stone wife
a penis red raw like a dog lipstick
and a wife that never sings.

Stubble

If I had stubble today,
I wish I had stubble today,
I'd have a piss patch in my trouser crutch,
hard rough hands to touch.

If I had stubble today,
I wish I had stubble today,
I would make a bet or two on a horse,
lose all my rent on whiskey of course,
slap my woman if the mashed potatoes got cold,
yell at my sons to do as they are told.

If I had stubble today,
I wish I had stubble today,
I would shag the landlord's wife,
get barred from that pub for the rest of my life.
I'd piss in the letterboxes of anyone who ever pissed me off,
put my sweaty balls in the hands of a nurse and cough.

If I had stubble today,
I wish I had stubble today,
I would flash my hairy dick in an old raincoat,
make a pearl necklace around a young slender throat.
I'd drink with the most magnificent thirst,
then lazy-sweat-fuck until I came first.

If I had stubble today,
I wish I had stubble today,
I may not have stubble on my face today,
I lost on the horses, my vest stinks and it's grey,
I've drunk loads of beer and there's vodka on the way,
I beat my lover to give me my own way all day.

Who needs stubble to be a cunt?

Dead Drunk

I tripped over a dead drunk, dead drunk.

I was blind drunk, blinded by rain and whiskey. I accidentally kicked him in the ribs. His wet raincoat fell open revealing a nest of cockroach-like beetles, which scuttled over his body, scrambling into the damp darkness of the creases of his layered clothes.

I tripped over a dead drunk, dead drunk.

How long he had been there I didn't know. He was drenched and he stank.

I tripped over a dead drunk, dead drunk.

He was lying in a doorway, the wrong way and twisted. I almost kicked him in the head; it was lucky I just got him in the side.

I tripped over a dead drunk, dead drunk.

We were both dead drunk. He was dead with drink and I was alive with drunk. His red blistered eyes were sealed blank, wet with teary raindrops. I tried to sit him up. I tried to help him. I am so sorry about that, I choked, I tripped I really didn't see you there.

I tripped over a dead drunk, dead drunk.

Once I got him upright with his back to the shop window, I lit two fags and put one in his slack mouth. I sat by him a while, took a good slug, and then put the half of whiskey in his cold hand. I wished him gentle things, so sorry about that my friend, I will see you again.

I tripped over a dead drunk, dead drunk.

I staggered towards the light of an open bar, an oasis in a desert of black sea taxis, hot dog vendors, pissed-up suits and the clip-clop of shop mannequins holding each other up by Wonderbra straps.

I tripped over a dead drunk, dead drunk.

And the bar was full of careless laughter. I hitched myself onto a bar stool and groped in my pockets for some money, sure I had some somewhere. I ordered a small beer and large whiskey, sat and smoked, soaked. I thought I tripped over a dead drunk, dead drunk.

I tripped over a dead drunk, dead drunk.

Dead drunk and homeless, I thought of those shiny beetles and the wet sleeping bag, the stench of hot dogs, the rain and piss soggy clothes, being hungry and cold. Being blind drunk, blinded by drink and rain, dead blind and drunk, drunk dead blind, dead drunk in a doorway.

I tripped over a dead drunk, dead drunk.

And I looked around the bar at the fuckwits and gutter sluts, the cunts and shit-for-brains. It was Animal Farm, all wankers are equal, but some wankers are more equal than others.

I tripped over a dead drunk, dead drunk.

I watched the bald dwarf landlord ogle the bar-lady with the greasy tits wibbling her cleavage into emptying an ashtray. She was a human rubbery fag-butt with grey ash eyes, her fingers were stained yellow and her hair was stinking tar and the colour of dry tobacco fields.

I tripped over a dead drunk, dead drunk.

And I contemplated the cost of fear of death, the cost of fear of life, the cost of dead drunk and drinking death, the cost of alive and living and the dues we pay. The differences between loneliness and the being alone.

I tripped over a dead drunk, dead drunk, I sat in a doorway in the rain with a dead drunk.
For dead drunk I may be, but not as drunk as he,
for he was dead, dead,
dead, drunk.

Ding! Dong! The Bells Are Gonna Chime

On Sunday
we watched the television,
there were silver-haired politicians
on the news who looked like
they had long forgotten
the thrill or the rush of blood,
of anything remotely resembling
passion and life and with hearts
as still as graves and eyes
all stone and moss.

They delivered a petition to No. 10 against equal marriage.

One ancient war-botherer
told us all at home
that he was against gay people in love
making weddings and making home
and making love love love.
And that boiled pink ham of a
man, he had quite an opinion.
I saw his eyebrow twitch.
He was that one cave man
that froze to death
denying the invention of-f-f-f
caves.

He may as well have been signing a petition
demanding the east winds be put in jam jars
to stop any wheel ever turning
to stop corners being so cornery
to make the round peg fit into the square hole
to stop the flowers of change and colour and
light and beauty and love and freedom and choice
ever blossoming.

I Don't Do Love

I don't do love, she once said.

She said bold as you like, bold as axis bold as love, she said I don't
do love. What she meant to say was I don't do love, love does me.
There are no defences, no boundaries, no rabbit-proof fences, just
all this stupid love doing me over and over again. Doing me when I
peel tomatoes, doing me when I hear a seagull, doing me whenever I
find evidence of a certain kind.

Love does me when I am trying to sleep. My dreams reek of the
acridity and absurdity, the fragility and mortality of love, the life of
love. Love does me constant and relentless, it's as if love has nothing
better to do with its time than work its grimy magic on me. It's a
syphilitic rash no cream will soothe.

I don't do love, she had said, and with such conviction that for a
breath she believed it herself. Until she looked and saw whom she
was saying it to. She said it like a knee-jerk comment in her internal
dialogue but then she blurted it as if it were the truth, as if it were
the time, as if it were a fact nobody would question or dissuade.

Love did her then, exactly when she said that.

When she said I don't do love, love did her hard and fast, love
pummelled without surcease. Love chewed at her throat, love ripped
at fistfuls of her hair and love pinned her against a piss-drenched
alleyway wall and love took her roughly. Love put her over his
lovely knee and love gave her a lovely spanking. Then love threw
back his lovely head and love belly-laughed at his trick. Now love
had her in a head-lock she'd never get out of. She was wrestling love
and love drop-kicked her.

She took some milk to try to feed and fill that hole love makes. She
prepared breadcrumbs so if she got lost in love she might find her
way home again, which were inevitably eaten by lovebirds. She
tried the antidotes, she read that ladybirds make you forget, but
love made the idea of eating a ladybird repulsive. Love told her the
ladybird had enough problems what with her house being on fire
and the children all gone.

Hope and belief were soon to follow. How do you put up a fair fight with love and hope and belief doing you relentless all night? Gangbanged by that holy trinity, the three of them at the same time, you don't stand a chance and it's enough to put you off your stroke, like the incessant phone, but of course it is never going to be love. Love don't ring to say love's on its way, love forces you to be patient, love lets you sweat a bit, but you can never sweat the love sickness out.

Soon love kicked down the doors and crashed through the walls with all love's doubts and fears and love's cynics and critics, with all love's confusions and responsibilities and love's champions and cheerleaders. Love threw a party, she was the host but she wasn't even invited.

It's like being a big brown bear with fleas but it itches inside your chest where no finger can reach and just like that big brown bear scratching against a rock, even some diversion like a quick lowering of standards will not suffice, nothing scratches that itch or eases the qualm.

I don't do love, I said, and when I looked up and saw just who I had said it to love did me hard and tirelessly, until, there was no until, there was just love.

Thunderbird Caravan

On the train from Ashford to Hastings
you will pass yellow fields
lily pond and tuft and matted sheep.
As you approach Ham Street
you'll notice a pig farm,
a line of tin-roofed shacks
that you cannot mistake
but I did.
I fell in love there once.
I was up to the neck in the swill.
We lived in that rusting, mildewed caravan
and we showered there
under a hose in that very meadow
whilst piglets snuffled in our hay bale furniture.
The sky and the time was summer,
we had bonfires and we had Neil Young,
we drank Thunderbirds under naked starlight.
I was skinny and barefoot and wild.
I was slapped and I got bruised.
I was sixteen and cocksure
but I had no idea how to come or go
until I ran away one dark night
through fields of corn.
I was once the prodigal daughter
shivering in the station
waiting for the dawn train
never knowing that years later
I'd be on a train to Hastings
leaning out of the window
looking for the pig farm
remembering
the sting of young love
remembering Harvest
a man needs a maid
are you ready for the country
heart of gold
the needle and the damage
done.

Can't Be Bovvered

Of course it's difficult! That's the whole point, tell me something I don't know, if it was easy everybody would do it, you CAN'T, that is the point of hard and difficult things. What is the point of doing something easy? What is easy? Is it easy being a CAN'T? Or a bank robber or a pilot or a heroin addict or a lion tamer or a millionaire? Is it easy to be honest or to be first? Anything worth doing is hard and worth doing really hard and for hours and every day until you have it down and you have done it the best you CAN otherwise it's pointless doing it, you CAN'T. Even being a total CAN'T takes hard work, hours of dedication and you should know that, you CAN'T. Every day you are shown evidence against being a CAN'T but every day you persist in being a total CAN'T, you lie there in your hot little bed planning what you CAN'T do or CAN'T say next.

If CAN'T s like you had your own way no books, songs or paintings would ever be completed because it might be a wee bit of work. Hello my name is Jimi Hend... dunt matta... Hello my name is Ludwig van Bee... bovvered. May as well stay in bed picking your nose and wiping it off on the sheets because it dunt matta wotevaaa, CAN'T be bovvered, CAN'T be bovvvered... I had a dream... yeah woteva. Romeo, Romeo, wherefore art... CAN'T be bovvered. If it was left up to you churches would be left half built and Neil Armstrong would be still on the moon waiting for a ride home and people would die in the middle of CAN'T be bovvered brain surgery and Jesus Christ would be left hanging there from one hand because it was a bit hard and it took a bit of energy to get the nail in through the palm of the other one, might as well leave it, just leave the son of God dangling by one arm, you CAN'T, now look the son of God just snapped at the wrist, headbutted his old dear and bloodied her nose because you, you sloppy CAN'T, you didn't even hammer that one in properly, you have a break, go on, dunt matta, dunk your Kit Kat.

CAN'T be bovvered going to galleries or reading books, dunt matta, you want pizza and lots of telly, you shit what you are fed... telly about telly, footage of fat ugly people bickering and scoffing pizza, you are watching yourself on telly, you CAN'T. How much imagination must it take to convince yourself that anything difficult, anything that takes a bit of thought or work must be avoided and ignored until someone on telly tells you it's kinda like pizza and worth checking out?

Once upon a time when you were a baby CAN'T it was very hard, very difficult to learn to stand and then to walk and even a CAN'T like you managed that... then it was hard and difficult to learn to speak CAN'T, and you speak CAN'T fluently, like it must be your first language. Then it was very hard, very difficult to learn to read and to write, to build ideas, to understand theories, histories and create things, and that's where CAN'T's like you stop whilst the rest of the world evolves and involves in spite of itself... in spite of you, you CAN'T. Outside it's filthy with life, with new ideas and a curiosity of how the world works and spins with the weight of thinking, questioning, the perfection of gifts and talents and finding fantastic ways to communicate dreams and visions, it's called seeing things through, you CAN'T, it's being alive and awake, you CAN'T. Paint a church ceiling? Paint a church ceiling, you sure? Oooooh, that will be very very hard, very very difficult, I wouldn't bovver if I was you, wotevaaa, your name is, ermmm, Michelangelo... woteva, Sistine Chapel... dunt matta... woteva... CAN can can can can can can can can can can... you CAN'T.

The Rosemary Branch

There you'll find me,
absent-minded wipe of the coffin-lid bar,
sucking Marlboros.
Number 108 on the jukebox jumps, skips.
Rain puddles reflect neon pink flashing.
I flash that bubbly barmaid smile.
Look, I don't make the prices up, I just pour them.
It's a business doing your pleasure with you.
Same again. Barflies don't ever give up licking taps.
What's the worst chat-up line I ever heard?
He winks, and I have to laugh out loud
because that has to be it.

There you'll find me
and there's the cabbie and the postman
discussing the state and the refugees.
It always ends with the singsong phrase,
that chorus about 'taking our jobs and the taxpayers' money'.
Refugees from their wives, they get them in anyway.
Naturally you can talk about yourself and recite Dylan.
That's a pint of Old Bob, not Thomas.
He asks me if I ever tried to get published.
Says I should speak to Roger McGough!
Asks if I ever heard of Benjamin Zephaniah.

There you'll find me,
and was it your sister in here last week?
Drank straight whiskey all morning with two builders,
which she left with, returned three hours later
with grass in knotted hair, looking for her shoe.
I thought that must have been your twin sister, right?
Daydreams are distracting, there's a moody sky over Angel.
I under-pour your wine, it's not up to the mark, sorry, I agree,
just not quite up to the mark, sure, you need Slimline Tonic,
darling, that amount of gin makes you grin, like it's funny,
double chin, funny as Czech beer no judge can pronounce.

There you'll find me,
and you ask for a pint of Pride
staring at my proud chest
and we all know this has nothing to do
with pride as I down the shot you got me
swallowed in one.
Nobody can be that proud.
Hair of the dog that you bit, bite first.
The pub quiz is as testing as it gets.
You've been hounding me like a Baskerville
and you clearly never read any Conan Doyle, Sherlock.

There you'll find me,
I am trying service with a trying smile,
whilst you talk on your mobile,
one eye on the football,
one eye on the dollar,
and your third eye on the score.
Top it up love. Top it up love.
Topping it up, slopping out,
flopping out of a low-cut nothing
from the market, cheap, nothing
is for free, nothing is for something,
money for nothing and your chicks are beer…

There you'll find me,
gently allowing my eyes to blur out of focus,
so slowly pouring the Guinness,
looking for the glint of ruby
in the bottom of the swirling stir
of disturbed swollen riverbeds.
There you'll find me, find me,
inhaling the rain in your air from the outside,
a pool of eve-light spills, reflects off Regent's Canal,
hot glasses steam in wet puddles on the coffin-lid bar.
There I will find you, as you will find me,
smiling, in an absent-minded bubble like I just pour them.

The Cricket

Tonight I'm sharing my room
with a lime green cricket,
he's a drama queen
in a panic inside the shade
of the bedside lamp.

He's a self-harming gothic.
He thumps his face on the bare bulb
and burns his eyes on the hot glass,
I try to catch him to set him outside
but he's too quick for me.

The mountains are lively tonight
and the white moon bears down
keeping us all awake.
The moon is blue-sunlight,
intimidating and filling me with fear.
I light a cigarette
and step onto the balcony
into pools of toxic mercury.

I feel the moon's frequency
vibrating and making
all creatures
fuck and fight
all night long.
I hear them caterwauling,
hot and itchy and sizzling
in the distant mountain range.

A lonesome dog howls,
warthogs bother a bin,
fat bats are black seagulls,
I hear a wild horse get wilder.
Lizards crawl up the white walls
and tap on the window
with rolling bloody eyes.

Mosquitoes lick their lips.
I wrap myself in the bed sheet
catching my ghostly reflection
in the window pane.

I change the subject
and try to think of the ocean,
and picture seahorses mating,
then I begin to list all sea life
that only do it on full moon.

But neither of us
are getting any tonight –
my suicidal roommate
has gone under my bed
to soothe his burnt eyeballs
and cry himself to sleep.

Self-piteous runt!
I just hope he won't
jump onto my face
out of spite
or sexual tension.

Insomniac –
the pair of us.
And below my balcony
mountain creatures
howl and cry and scream
they kill themselves and
murder each other
with love for the
merciless
hot white
moon.

Blackbird

I start writing at 4am
when bony branches tap
against the starlight.
I'm listening to one
January bird
singing a hungry,
cold, dawn song,
and it's then I think
I love you,
you,
there in the bed as
you turn softly
to feel me go.
Shush, I say.
Go back to sleep.

I leave your warmth
to shiver at my desk
and write this poem
about now and January
and the blackbird
and the tapping of branches
against first light.
I'm capturing this hour
in my tea cup.

I write
I love him because
when I ask for his advice
he never suggests
the easy or cheap route
the fast or smooth path
always it's the big thing to do

he says
look for the big thing to do
and it's often difficult but
he's often right.

It's 7am when
I put down my pen
and slide back into bed,
I hold him close and
feel him stir and rise,
there he is and there we are,
it's the start of the day
the beginning of a new year
and love is the big thing
to do.

The Good Stuff

I haven't spoken
for three days
to a person.
I spoke to a fly
cunt,
I told it to
fuck off,
and then
I spoke to myself,
I said
stupid wanker
as I went downstairs
without the thing
I went upstairs for…

There are days
when the blood in my brains
drains somewhere else,
the energy shifts,
maybe I am
popping an egg,
I have a low battery,
no inspiration,
and it's 38 degrees
in the merciless sun.
I've been silent
such a long time.
Yesterday!
Ah yesterday,
you should have met me
yesterday,
I was a champion.
I got up at 4am,
before the sun rose,
and wrote
solid
writing,
the good stuff,
the stuff you get lost in
and it was 4pm
when I stopped writing.

I must have needed to
drink or eat or piss
or look at a bird
but I felt like I had
accomplished
good stuff,
put in the time,
a good
twelve hours'
hard labour.

Today
I am not a champion,
today
I am a wanker.

There is
nothing new
going on inside,
my heart is diluted,
I am that flat glass
of Coca-Cola
that was left in the sun
with a scum of
diluted ice
on its surface.

I drink coffee
and smoke
check Facebook
erase every
status update
I attempt
and annoy myself.

It is tense
between
me and me,
we are not talking.

All I want is
a little whinge
a little attention
to hear my name
said with familiarity
some laughs and
some good stuff.

It's all very well
sitting here in my pants
with my brown boobs,
doing solitude
up a mountain
at a writers' retreat
alone and shit

but I sure could
use a smile or
a pat on the head and
then I would gladly skip
happily back to my stories
the notebooks
and the poems.

I'd embrace
this silence and
the solitude
this
and that
like yesterday like that
good stuff.

Cathedrals

Each morning we build cathedrals, we decorate them with sea shells and eyelash salt, warm light and dreams of butterflies.

But by nightfall nothing remains but trampled sand castles, coppery, tarnished green, a fear of the night that drowns us, then the sea that washes it away.

Each morning we build cathedrals, we decorate them with gold dust and sea salt kisses, chocolates and silver rings and summer things and dreams of flying flowers.

But by nightfall nothing remains but a tramp and his dog pissing in winter's doorway, a fear of the fear as the blood of Friday night washes us away.

Each morning we build cathedrals, we decorate them with violet dawn light and dreams of flying, and dreams of dreams of flying.

But by nightfall nothing remains but a list of things to do and a mesh of things unanswered, and the dreadful knowledge that we are not what we intend to do – we are what we already did, intentionally.

And each morning we build cathedrals, this one is made of sandpaper, we decorate it with glitter, phosphorus and ribbons, we ink and hand-print our best intentions, we brush it with milk and prick it with a fork and bake it.

But by dusk, nothing remains but a rusty caravan, empty balloons are ripped condoms, there's the fear of the plump shadow, and the vodka and the cunts wash all your wishes down, with the laughter like a drain.

This morning you built a cathedral, you rose, you bloomed with prick, kick and thorns, this one has a thick skin of rubber, it will be as soft and yielding as time, forgiving and elastic as love, love, over and over again love, over and over again.

The N-word

If that word were a man,
would that word stand tall?
Would that word be your equal?
Would that word sound grand?
If that word were a woman,
would that word be your girlfriend?
Would that word be educated?
Would that word understand?
If that word were your king,
would that word be fair?
Would that word have grace?
Would that word rule the land?
If that word were a child,
would that word be joyful?
Would that word feel the sting
of the back of your hand?
And if that word were a dog,
would that word come to heel?
Would that word eat off your floor?
Would that word bite your hand?
And if that word is a river,
is it polluted by you?
And if that word is a clock,
did you stop time too?
And if that word is a cage,
do you have the keys?
And if that word is a forest,
can you see the wood for the trees?

That word is the N-word.
Do you use it with shame?
Do you use that name because
you don't understand?
You spread ignorance and fear
like a million wet grains of sand.
Every time I hear the word Nigger,
that word is a gun
loaded with negativity and history,
blood 'n' fire and truth run,
sticks and stones may break my bones
but names will always hurt thee.
If that word were a flag
I'd burn it happily
because we still have slavery
in the 21st century.
If that word had a soul
I would set her free.
If that word had a soul I say
set them free.
And if that word is the word
you'd use to describe me,
I say set me free, set me free,
set me free.

Her Indoors

On good days
I hear movement and music
and her bathwater running
by at least midday.

On bad days I see her
shivering in her pyjamas
and Wellington boots
buying vodka at 10am.

On good days I smell cooking,
I observe her shopping
fresh vegetables from the market,
I see her with flowers and a spring in her step,
she opens her windows wide
and puts geraniums on the sill,
I overhear the industrial crash and bang of life,
a party of laughter and surprises,
champagne corks popping and stuck records
and I hear men's deep voices in there too,
I hear the bed posts banging against the wall
and the sound of love being thrown around the rooms.

But today must be a bad day,
all I hear is the tapping of the death-watch beetle,
the funereal murmur of the shipping forecast,
there's a smell of burnt toast and stale smoke,
the curtains are closed again,
they'll stay shut all day today,
there is an intermittent sound of typing.

She is alone in there
with her ghosts and doubts.
I haven't heard her phone ring for days.
I heard her moan and call out.
It could have been an orgasm or
it could have been weeping.
Maybe she hurt herself.

I used to like to see her striding out at dusk
bouncing gaily in red shoes and scarlet lipstick
her hair aflame with curls and life
but no.
Not for a while.

Maybe she's bipolar or
alcoholic or a manic depressive,
maybe someone died
or something got killed,
it would be better if it was a something,
then maybe she could get some help.
I think she needs help.

Because this time
the stench of silence has gone on and on.
I don't hear parties or love or guitars out of tune.
I don't even hear the toilet flush
or see her take her rubbish out
and her post is left unopened
by the front door.

I don't hear the click of her red shoes.
Her high heels are stored in boxes
for best of times and for good times.
When I hear them again
it will be like the first cuckoo
and the pink cherry blossom,
the return of laughter and
happy days.

I sit on the end of her bed
waiting for her to come back.

Mae West

If you can't go straight, you've got to go around.

She was a fast-moving woman
who liked to take it slow,
it was not the men in her life
but the life in her men.

When she landed in London
they asked Ms West,
How do you like Big Ben?
She said she was disappointed
he was just a clock.

Her problem was never how much sex she had
but how much she could get away with –
submitting hot scripts loaded with lines she knew would be cut,
she'd save the real script until shooting or first night and then
watch the studio managers and theatre bosses go white with fear
but change their minds quick when the queues grew and tickets
sold out.

She was the first woman to dance the shimmy live on stage,
a provocative move she picked up in late night clubs,
speakeasies and ghettos, consorting with poor white trash and
coloured folk.
And when Duke or Louis played – they really played –
she wouldn't allow Hollywood bosses to pay white guys
to mime their tunes to camera.

Her life's work was a revolt against censorship,
whipping up a frenzy in redneck Bible belts
and challenging moralising bigots.
She wrote scandalous scripts –
a black man kissing a white woman and also a gay kiss.
And spent her life on the road and touring
whilst writing plays, books and live shows.
She was born in the 1890s
and didn't get to the silver screen and Hollywood
or become a real household name
until she was over forty years old.
She once booked a cast of down and out homeless bums,
she gave them shelter and paid work
whilst creating an authentic Harlem ghetto on stage
and it was a sell-out show.

She dated fit boxers and sportsmen,
perhaps because they could keep up with her stamina.
She had a voracious sexual appetite
fuelling gossip she must be hermaphrodite
but she was one hundred per cent woman.

She enjoyed sex,
but like an athlete in training
she abstained when she was working.

She believed in sexual freedom
but never screamed off the rooftops,
rather whispered to one man at a time.
As she said –
Goodness has nothing to do with it,
there are no good girls gone wrong
just bad girls found out.

She reduced Cary Grant to a whimper,
when her male co-star reached to hold her hand
she said through smouldering eyes,
It ain't heavy, I can carry it for myself.

They used to call me Saliva as in spit,
the stuff you use to polish a thing
when you are all out of elbow grease.
And, well, whoever said somebody said
there is a book inside everybody
was inside a somebody at the time.

So, peel me a grape!
The only difference
between you and me, honey,
is you can afford to give it away.

Throw discretion to the wind
and your hips to the north,
south, east and west.
There's not a dry seat in the house
for the legendary
Mae West.

The Colony Poem
For Michael Wojas

I don't know what to wear
to your funeral today
something black
something pinstripe
something green
something gay
a bottle of vodka breath
and my knickers the wrong way
I don't know what to wear
to your funeral today
an ashtray around my neck
paint my nails lime
a pair of mirrored shades
to hide the tears of tearing time
a magpie on my shoulder
a bacon on my back
a skull and crossbones flag
leopard-skin sling backs
because
whenever you were nice to me
it meant the fucking world to me
and when you gave me vodka free
it meant the fucking world to me
and when you gave me money for a taxi
to make sure I'd get home safely
it meant the fucking world to me
it meant the fucking world to me
and when you listened to my CD
and pressed play whenever you saw me
it meant the fucking world to me
that meant the fucking world to me
and when you put my band posters in the lavatory
and my poems on the bar for all to see
it meant the fucking world to me
that meant the fucking world to me
and that you did this complimentary
it was not obligatory
and it meant the fucking world to me
it meant the fucking world to me
I recognised your generosity
Michael of the Colony

because
it meant the fucking world to me
it meant the fucking world to me
and I don't know what to wear
to your funeral today
something black
something pinstripe
something green
something gay
bottle of vodka breath
and my knickers the wrong way
and to all tomorrow's parties
raise a glass to yesterday
to all the good times
the good people
at your funeral
today.

Pride and Prejudice

This morning I noticed the sky was a baggy story.
I reached up to pull at a flappy bit of old argument.
It was a tired and clammy cloud.
It was wallpaper from an old protest that was never resolved,
merely brushed aside until she pulled her burnt bra on to make the tea.
Before long I had peeled it all away in strips
and once that corner of sky was torn
behind the story and underneath
there was just the opaque roof of a department store elevator.
I wanted to pull the slats apart, to climb up into the lift shaft
and then cut the ropes and watch Twitter world crash.

And off-line and off-grid
we were all fish out of water
slapped onto the cold pavement
and we stopped compulsive likelikelike button pushing,
opened the curtains to daylight to celebrate
our differences and our sameness
and seeing the barriers all shattered
we were forced to go outside
to walk and work side by side.

Because we won't remember the twitter trolls
or the twitter troll slayers
but the bully-goat bridge that we built to shelter them.
Just as I don't recall the names of playground bullies
but the classmates that took detention by my side
and with a sinking feeling, I remember the girls
that fingered their blonde plaits and stood by and watched.
We are plugged into a distraction and logged into fiction,
counting sheep and followers
when our dreams are so much more,
more than we ever gave them credit for.
We are sleep-walking, sleep-talking, retweeting parrots.
We keep poking and fiddling with the knobs
like it's the only way to sound check our speakers

And we'll still argue –
because a woman cannot choose to be silent if she had no voice,
because the invisible women that have no votes have no choice,
because silence is gold but it's kept in a bank,
because there are so many inspiring women to thank and to rank,
because it isn't just 140 characters, it's your motive and intent,
because Twitter is real life and you tweet, threatened and sent.

One word from you shall silence me forever.

That's Jane Austen
and there's two words.

Pride and Prejudice.

A Strong and Stiffly Worded Letter Should Do the Trick

Dear war makers and war takers,
twitchy button pushers and mushroom cloud worshippers,
bomb botherers and gun polishers,
chemical weapon wielders and coup-cooers,
battle cry criers and army gatherers,
bullet loaders and knife sharpeners,
death collators, chief whips and spins and
dear kings and dear lords and dear right honourables.
To all the dear Mr Presidents and dear Mr Prime Ministers –

Thank you for taking some time to read this letter.
I am writing to make a small request –
please could you all just take a fucking day off?
Go to the park, feed the ducks, read a book.
Take a break and put down your war-stirring spoons.
Shush with your fighting talk. Stop with your itchy button-pushy fingers.
Quit being so trigger-happy.
Give your eye-for-an-eye campaign a rest.

Just take some time out –
do your laundry, water your plants, visit your mother,
pull a sickie, have a duvet day, watch a whole season of *Breaking Bad*
but just stop.

I suggest you all turn off your phones,
unplug your internet and take a breather.
Stop winding each other up. I don't care who started this trouble.
You're all as bad as each other. I want to send you to your rooms
to do your homework –
you all need to read the history books
and refresh your geography.

So here's the thing:
If you could just stop making bombs. And you, if you could stop
pretending you haven't sold any bombs. And then if you could stop
pretending you haven't bought any bombs. And then you, if you could
stop threatening to bomb people that would be brilliant. Yeah. If you
could all stop threatening us with all your bombs that you haven't built or
sold or bought that would be terrific. Hang on. Let me put it another way,
simplify things: if you could stop making bombs and you stop selling
bombs and if you could stop bombing people and if you could all stop
threatening us all with bombs all the fucking time that would be brilliant.

One more time, let me put it another way: if you could stop making bombs and you stop selling bombs to the other side when you are meant to be on the other side, and if you could stop accusing the other one of having the bombs, whilst procuring the production of more bombs, which you know the latter has because you have the receipts because it was you who fucking ordered them in to be manufactured and sold them in the first fucking place... that would be great.

Now go and have a fucking cup of tea and do a crossword.
Do something lovely and ordinary with your time.
Bake a fucking cake or something.
Since you have all this surplus energy and money
for bombs and war planes,
go and build a school or a hospital or save the rainforests
or something useful.
Put all that war chest money into grants towards that cure for cancer.

Save a soldier, save some money, send him home.

There is not one person I know wants to see another
human being killed.
I certainly don't want anyone shot or blown up, how ludicrous.
And you always end up bombing schools and hospitals and
killing children and women, because your aim is crap.
At least we are all to believe that it's because your aim is crap.

Now climb off your war horses and stop yelling charge.
It's repetitive and it's pissing us all off.
Seriously, I think I can safely say
you are pissing everyone off
with the constant fighty-talk.
I just had to switch Radio 4 off, yet again.
It was vibrating with all the chest beating.
My radio was filled with a bunch of silverback gorillas.
Stop with the King Kong method.

What is it with all the killy-killy-bomb talk?
Are you all drunk or something?
Has your summer of *Get Lucky* gone a bit sour?
Stay up all night to get killy...
Stay up all night to get bomby...

159

Obama, Cameron, Putin, Bashar, Letta,
whips and spins and government war stirrers,
every one of you in every war bunker,
yes, you and you, all of you,
all of you, go to your rooms.
I think you need to go take a nap.

Start a war? Seriously? You are going to start a war?
Start a war? START A WAR? Bomb people?
Chemical weapons, bullets, minefields, bombs, all that good stuff…
Yep. That's your solution, is it?
You bag of hopeless dicks.

With Kindest Regards,
pretty much everyone.

I Found My Father

What a magnificent thing
I finally found Dad
I found out where he was buried
this very morning
and it's a relief and a sadness
right underneath me
the centre of me
I am sitting here
writing this
with the feeling
it's going to take one more push
one last bit of courage
and then I will go and see his final resting place
and say goodbye at last
and after all these years
of seeking and not knowing
somebody replied to my message
a random act and a long shot
a message in a bottle
left on an electronic beach
I learnt something today
something about belief
something about keeping going
something about trusting people
that there are people out there
who will put pen to paper and reply
so whatever you do today
do it well
do it like you mean it
it's all on its way
be careful what you wish for you may get it
be happy for what you wish for you will get it
what a thing to wake up to
what a rush of life
and death
and the nine-year-old inside me
the lost little girl is found
she is released like balloons
into the blue sky.

All We Can Do is Hope

All we can do is hope
that the people we love
could love us too,
that the people we want to spend time with
could make time to spend with us.

After all the hullabaloo
everything leaves its scratch and scar tissue,
you get altered and informed
by the people that come
and the people that go.

This constant metamorphosis
is the snake skin of your next decisions that will be shed
because there is no standing still, everything is changing,
there is only snatching time to be alone, to brush yourself down,
to see where you have landed this time, who you have landed as
and what you might like to do next, or later and with who, or not.

It is the nature of things to grow and change,
it is the wheel of fortune and fate,
of choices and happy accidents,
how wonderful and terrible at once,
it is both puzzling and a freedom,
sometimes we sit with the cage door wide open,
it is crippling and a responsibility
being wrong or right or both and there we find more choice
to have regrets or to feel guilty,
to judge or hold grudges or forget it or
take your time to heal or count your pieces of silver.

At sunset I look at the dirty canal water
reflecting drunks on stag nights in St Patrick's Guinness hats
slavering at the windows of the red light district.
I am meniscus – spilling with a realisation – I am not who I thought
I was.
I looked for myself but I was not there or here, not anymore,
it is the nature of things to grow and change,
I forgot that included me.

And now the whores look so young and half empty
the red-eyed sniggering Irish lads are not cute but an annoyance
the junky is a dead-eyed rat with his open-wound twitching
huddled over his flame by the bins.

I look at this wooden bridge.
I wonder how long that took to build
and how quickly we destroy bridges.
I hear my ghosts clattering against the cobbled stones
laughing – eighteen and out of my mind
crying – twenty-five and out of my mind
singing – twenty-eight and out of my mind
silence – thirty-three and in my mind.

I wonder when she got here, this woman.
I order a small beer and smoke alone in this Amsterdam bar.
I am brushing myself down to see where I have landed this time and
who as,
both exhausted and exhilarated by this question
because even stopping to write this
was a choice.

If I am ever found –
we should come to this bar
because this is the place where this poem was made
because all I ever could do was hope
because all we can do is hope.
All we can do is hope
that the people we love
can love us too.

The Good Cock

It was a good cock, there is no disputing it. It made her giddy just to look at it, throbbing, twitching and pulsating there in his hand. It made all women sigh, grunt and moan, of course, it made all other women crazy, but she wasn't thinking about all other women, for then and there, it was hers, it was a good cock and it was all for her. She was thinking about the good cock and the width of it, the thought of it, the view was spectacular. She wanted to see what it would feel like inside her, she wanted to feel what it would be like to have such a good cock. And she wanted it. It was thick and long, it was hard and it was all for her, for the then, and for the now. Just the sight of it made her ridiculous, she thought in songs: have you ever seen such a thing in your life, such a spectacular cock in all of your life? Hypnotic and red-faced it was, the cock had fury and hunger, a personality of its own, it was arrogant and primal. He held it back tightly. Then he lowered the front passenger seat and positioned himself on top of her. He was strong and quite heavy and she was pinned under his weight now. So the good cock let her have a taste and gave her a feel of some of the tip of it, just the very tip of the good cock. He gave her a quick lazy kiss, all tongue and spit as he worked the cock in. Then he gave her a few good and sudden strokes followed by a few good hard thrusts. She opened herself and moved with him and he said, don't do that or you'll make me come. So she stopped bucking and grinding and tried to be good for the good cock. She played dead and let the cock have its own wicked way. It was sharp and delicious, with each throb and stab the cock grew harder, more swollen. She was aware that she was making strange noises in her throat, normally she was quite quiet, but for now and for the good cock she was a whimpering girl, a virgin, he seemed to like it like that. Don't move, he gasped, or I will come, he said, don't move or I will come. So she had to stay perfectly still as he entered her again and again, teasing short spurts followed by slow full length of good cock, there in the front seat of the car, in the car park, outside the train station.

Suddenly he ducked his head down and he stopped moving momentarily because he could see a man walking his dog. He looked at the man walking his dog whilst he began to continue slowly fucking her. As though by doing it very slowly it would look less rude to the man and his dog. He looked at the man walking his dog and pushed himself back inside her hard, looking past her shoulder and through his rear window at the dog walker. She chuckled and this made her jiggle. He said, please don't do that, don't move or you will make me come. She stifled her giggling and stopped laughing and again she was very still. Her legs open and jammed up against the dashboard and her skirt up around her throat. The gear stick digging into her side.

This time though, when he was doing it to her, she plain lost her composure, she sighed then cried out in pleasure and pulled him into her. He didn't look into her face, he looked at his good cock going in and out and then over at the dog walker. He looked down and watched himself go in and out and then over at the dog walker, in and out, the dog walker and then in and out. She threw her arms around his neck and clenched and lifted herself onto him from below. She couldn't help it, she thrust herself back onto him. He was sweating as he looked at his cock and then he said oh oh oh. She bucked beneath him fiercely three or four or so times and she dug her nails through his denim jacket and bit into his collar, his neck and hair. Very suddenly, he clambered off her and out of the car door clasping the end of his cock. He had the foreskin pinched between his fingers and when he let go of the end, creamy sperm shot all over the front car tyre. She lay there watching him but she could only see him from the waist up. Out of her view he had one hand to steady himself on the roof of the car and the other on his good cock, his face grimaced slightly and his eyes were closed. She watched him and out of sight, out of frame, his come spurted against the car park tarmac and the front tyre.

She closed her legs and sat up, she found her knickers on the floor of the car and pulled them back on over her boots. She was relieved he didn't come inside her. She'd never seen such a good cock, inexplicable timing, coughing up against a car tyre like that too. She had been wondering where his sperm would go. She was expecting to get it rubbed into her belly and breasts, splashed into her face, squirted into her eyes where it stings... but it was much tidier this way. This way there would be no marks on her clothes or his car seat, no residue on her skin to reappear in the bath later. She straightened her skirt, pushed her right tit back in her bra and pulled her T-shirt back down. He drew breath whilst he did up his flies, then walked around and got back into the driving seat. They smiled at each other. They giggled about the man walking his dog, as he started the engine and patted her knee. The car had a sweet smell, sex, cheese, sweat, vanilla, beer and wheat. They opened the steamy windows and the air was cool. He drove to the other side of the car park, to the train station entrance and dropped her off for the 3pm train. They kissed, pecked each other goodbye and made noises to call each other some time and soon. It was sunny on the platform, golden light soaked the stony train tracks, she smoked a cigarette alone.

Ball-Ache

Last June –
it was my birthday.
The sky was perfectly blue.
I was as happy as you can ever be,
happy as a child in the warm Mallorcan sun.
The olive trees were bent and crooked,
the castle on the distant hill stood quiet,
the swimming pool rippled in gold morning sunlight
and sweet cherries bobbed on the surface of my champagne.
I was smoking and drinking and opening gifts and cards
when I noticed Richard was trembling
as he produced a box and lifted the lid
to reveal a sparkling ring.
Shiny diamonds winked at me,
and now my love, he was shaking and
I didn't hear what he was saying
with his mouth
because I was laughing and
this action speaks louder than any words
and my mouth was saying,
Ooh… just like a real girl,
my eyes were blurred with tears
and Ooh…
I kept saying,
Ooh...
and my ears were all bells and laughter
and somewhere bluebirds were singing
and somewhere else butterflies played trumpets
but all I could hear was
Ooh, until I blurted,
Dickie, are you asking me to be your official ball-ache?
Yes, Salena, I'm asking you to be my ball-ache.
Your official ball-ache… forever?
Yes, Salena, my official ball-ache, forever.
And with that we snogged and fell into a bundle of
laughing and crying and kissing,
the best kind of laughing and crying and kissing,
the kind of laughing and crying and kissing
that'll stick to your insides
every time you remember it,
the kind of laughing and crying and kissing
that'll stick to your insides every time.

Funny Thing Being a Writer

Most of the time you don't get to do any writing,
a lot of the time you wonder where the writing went.
Oftentimes you miss the writing,
and missing writing feels like racing with an absence of a horse
between your thighs,
or a wave crashing over your head,
or a sweet swallow, a taste in your throat,
or an ache in your chest that hurts.
Missing writing is a bit like missing a person,
but the person is inside of you.
And you pick up a pencil and your notebook,
looking for substance and worth,
for some sort of healing balm.
You know you only have an afternoon
or less, until you are required
not to write anymore
and that writing is hot,
that writing is like an affair.
It's a hard-motel-fuck of a write.
You make that time mean something
and you don't wash your hands after
so you can smell yourself on your fingers.
Then it's off back to the front of the factory,
dressing the shop windows, selling your wares.
You are the head chef of your own restaurant,
you've got hungry customers that need servicing,
got a commission in the oven waiting to rise,
and some of the good stuff chilling on ice.
Your larder is full of writings you did years ago though,
back when you were cold and poor and thin and wild,
when all you wanted to do was be a writer, when
all you ever did was dream and write, all day and all night and
nobody expected you to do anything else but write,
back then when you thought writing was all that writers had to do.

Thanks and acknowledgements

With special thanks to the legendary Jock Scot. Massive thank you to Clive Birnie and all my Burning Eye poetry comrades. Thank you to Oli Spleen, Kelly-Anne Davitt and Olivia Rutherford. Thanks to John Cooper Clarke and Tim Wells who encourage this sort of behaviour. With love to Richard Cripps and my Mum and family, to Piers, Hetty, Marcus, Peter, Sally, Dani, Cherie, Mel, Patty, Marcia and Lee. And lastly thank you to all the people that live in these poems, as you read this book please raise a glass to our absent friends, Emily, Michael, Gigi and Cheryl B.

Some of these poems were published or broadcast on... Resonance FM. BBC Radio 3. BBC Radio 4. BBC World Service. GLR. BBC LDN. BBC Scotland. Under The Pier, Nasty Little Press. Liminal Animal, Tongue Fu Anthology. Raconteur, Parthian Books. Dwang, Tangerine Press. The Salzberg Review. The Fire People Anthology, Canongate. Rising Magazine. The Illustrated Ape. The Dark Times. Trespass Magazine. Antique Children. Gargoyle. Artefiction. Paraphilia Magazine. Full Moon Empty Sports Bag. Saline Trips. SaltPetre Radio. The Decadent Handbook, Dedalus Books. Velocity, Black Spring Press. Connecting Something to Nothing, Influx Press. Bang Said The Gun Anthology, Burning Eye...and numerous zines, pirate radio stations and magazines.

Many of these poems were performed at... Hay-On-Wye Literary Festival. How The Light Gets In... The London Palladium. Wilderness Festival. Cornbury Festival. Voewood Festival. Aldeburgh Poetry Festival. Ubud Writers and Readers Festival, Indonesia. First Story Festival. Standon Calling. Port Eliot Festival. The Book Club Boutique, London. The Book Club Boutique Down Under. Dicks Bar. The House of St Barnabus. Blacks. The House Of Lords. Groucho's. The Colony Room. The Electric Picnic. Salon London. The Roundhouse. Nowhereisland. Norwich Fringe Festival. Galway. Cork. Dublin. Wave If You Are There, Liverpool. Camp Bestival. Speaky Spokey, Brighton. Stoke Newington Literary Festival. Hammer and Tongue. Book Slam. Tongue Fu. Bang Said The Gun. Neu Reekie. The Hackney Empire. Charlie Wrights. Out-Spoken. Do Lectures. The Secret Garden Party. The Royal Festival Hall. The Southbank. Warsaw Hard Rock Café, Poland. The Unfair Party Brussels. The Dartmouth Arms. The Rosemary Branch. The Clapham Grand. Latitude Festival. York Lesbian Arts Festival. Bestival, The Isle Of Wight. Foyles Bookshop. The Jazz Café. The Port Eliot Literature Festival. Cornelia Street Café New York. CBGB's and various bars and sleazy joints across the USA. FAK Festival Croatia. Underground Party Copenhagen. The Purcell Rooms. Edinburgh Fringe Festival. Bloomsbury Theatre. The Union Chapel. The Poetry Café. Glastonbury Festival. Reading Festival. The Crap Stage. Crossing Borders Festival, Amsterdam. Donuts, Berlin. Landestheater Austria. Palabras Festival of Literature and Music, Holland and Belgium. The Big Chill. Broomhill Art Hotel. The Enchanted Garden, Devon. 12 Bar. Mean Fiddler London. Filthy McNasty's. Vox & Roll, Arthrob. The Ministry Of Sound. Express Excess. The Hard Edge Club. Big Word. Apples and Snakes... and hundreds of graveyards, beach bars, campfires, pub lock-ins and always in the kitchen at parties.

Lightning Source UK Ltd.
Milton Keynes UK
UKOW01f1405050916

282221UK00001BA/51/P